Had Eve Come First
and Jonah Been a Woman

Had Eve Come First and Jonah Been a Woman

Nancy Werking Poling

RESOURCE *Publications* • Eugene, Oregon

HAD EVE COME FIRST AND JONAH BEEN A WOMAN

Copyright © 2010 Nancy Werking Poling. All rights reserved. Except for brief quotations in critical publications or reviews, no part of this book may be reproduced in any manner without prior written permission from the publisher. Write: Permissions, Wipf and Stock Publishers, 199 W. 8th Ave., Suite 3, Eugene, OR 97401.

Resource Publications
An Imprint of Wipf and Stock Publishers
199 W. 8th Ave., Suite 3
Eugene, OR 97401
www.wipfandstock.com

ISBN 13: 978-1-60899-739-8

Manufactured in the U.S.A.

For Jim

Thanks for years of listening as I worked out my own theology—weird and unorthodox as it's been. Your love helps me better understand God as a companion who cares, challenges, and forgives.

Contents

Preface ix
Acknowledgments xiii

Lonely Woman *(Garden of Eden)*	1
Survival *(Noah)*	4
Confused *(Tower of Babel)*	12
Not All Who Wander are Lost *(Abraham)*	14
The Lamb that Was Slain *(Isaac)*	23
Insubordination *(Isaac)*	27
Jabbok Night *(Jacob)*	30
When Sisters Dream *(Joseph)*	38
Better to Have Made the Journey *(Moses)*	47
The Wall *(Jericho's Walls)*	57
And You Will Eat of the Honey *(Samson)*	61
The Road to Ramah *(Samuel)*	68
Let None of Us Be Cowards *(David and Goliath)*	75
As She Loved Her Own Soul *(David and Jonathan)*	80
The Mentor *(Elijah and Elisha)*	86
More than a Woman Can Bear *(Job)*	94
A Sisterhood of Survivors *(Shadrach, Meshach, and Abednego)*	102
The Nice Woman *(Jonah)*	109

Preface

WHEN I was a child, my parents read to me from *Hurlbut's Story of the Bible*, a 723-page volume I still own. Later I read for myself the many stories that were to instruct me. I kept trying to understand the lessons I was supposed to be learning, for I sincerely wanted to grow up to be a good woman.

But some of the narratives never made sense. In Genesis, for instance, I worried about the story of Cain and Abel. Why was God so picky about whether people sacrificed animals or plants? If God was a *loving* father, why had he deliberately flooded the earth and killed the people and animals? And there was the story of Jacob, who cheated his brother out of his birthright. I had been taught not to lie or cheat, yet Jacob seemed to have been rewarded for both. David killed a giant. Wasn't killing a sin?

Not until midlife did it occur to me that Bible stories were men's stories. As a girl, I was not supposed to identify with the heroes. Neither literally nor metaphorically was I supposed to lead my people, slay giants, wrestle with angels, or have a special relationship with God.

Nowadays preachers search the scriptures for biblical women, lifting them up for illustration: Ruth, Hagar, Deborah, Esther, Rahab among them. A few, such as Deborah, are the central character of a story, but nearly always men get the exciting roles while women make up the supporting cast. Biblical times were, after all, quite different from our modern era.

Yet the ancient stories can speak eloquently to women struggling with contemporary issues: leading victims of violence to a safe place (Moses); starting a new life in an unfamiliar land (Abraham); selling our sister/brother into slavery (Joseph's brothers); God despairing over the corruption of humanity (Noah and the flood).

These observations led me to wonder, how might the story of Noah been different had he been a woman? Had Moses been born female, whom might she have rescued and led?

As a result of my musings, I felt inspired to rewrite some of the old favorites, using women as the main characters. At first I feared taking blasphemous liberties, but then remembered preachers' variations on the themes: Jeremiah as a twentieth-century man, taking on the corporations; Job as the man who is unemployed, and his wife has left him, and the mortgage payment is due; Noah as the man mocked by his Midwestern suburban neighbors for heeding God's instructions to build a submarine. So why not imagine some of the protagonists as women?

I am not a biblical scholar. I am a story teller, bringing my imagination to many of the situations and characters I grew up hearing about. So I have not gone back to original texts (not that I have the ability to), but read and reread passages from modern translations. In some cases I have loosely followed the biblical narrative, trying to capture the tone an elder storyteller might have used around an evening fire. At other times I have veered more boldly from the text. In a few cases, as with the bond between David and Jonathan, I have decided there is power in simply substituting women for men and letting the story stand.

When I finished writing this collection, I realized that the God I have imagined differs in many ways from the one I have heard about most of my life. The God on these pages is flexible, able to listen and be dissuaded. As my daughter pointed out, like many an effective CEO, God may value those who challenge more than those who meekly follow orders.

As much as I wanted God always to be benevolent, I was not able to bring my own wishes to every text. Just as God's actions in Hebrew scripture can be harsh and undeserved, women too are not consistently moral and upright people. So not every story leaves us loving God or women more.

To better discern the parallels, you might want to first turn to the Bible passage on which each narrative is based. Or you may simply choose to read the stories for their own sake. In either case, I hope they speak to you in a way that affirms your experience and inspires you to probe the relationship between God and Woman.

Acknowledgments

During part of the 1980s and 1990s, I was blessed to be associated with the women of Downtown United Presbyterian Church, Rochester, New York. Under the leadership of pastors Rose Mitchell and Gail Ricciuti, we met regularly for a Sunday evening gathering called Women, Word, and Song. I continue to value the way each woman in that group touched my life and inspired me to open my mind to new and meaningful images of God.

My thanks, too, to longtime friends Jeannine Steiner and Verna Todd for doing what good friends do: affirming my gifts and encouraging me to write from the heart.

I am grateful for advice from two scholars: Dr. Phyllis Bird, who advised me on how I might feminize male names, and Dr. Rosemary Radford Ruether, who read the manuscript in an early stage. However, any inaccuracies of biblical times or characters are entirely my responsibility.

Fortunately, my husband, Jim, hasn't kept a tally of the times I've interrupted his own writing to think out loud about mine. His theological training and feminist perspective, not to mention his patience, have been a tremendous resource.

Lonely Woman

Genesis 1 & 2

God creates Man, placing him in the Garden of Eden.
Had she been created first, might Woman have felt one with the earth and animals rather than compelled to subdue creation?

Hurled through the heavens, spinning, spinning, spinning with the upheaval of creative force, Woman landed with a thump upon the earth. From non-being to being, just like that.

Dazed, she lay awhile hoping the crick in her neck would soon go away. And the muscle spasms in her back. After complaining to Creator that surely there was a gentler way to come into life—which Creator disputed, insisting that creativity is a painful process for both Creator and created—Woman fell asleep.

A chorus awakened her. Melodious chirps and tweets and coos, all in praise of Creator. Gazing upward, she saw feathered creatures, some bold in color, others in hues so similar to their surroundings they could hardly be seen. Many were perched on delicate branches that peacefully swayed.

Standing on shaky legs, Woman lifted her arms, waving them back and forth in imitation of the branches. As she tried to join the joyful song, she was startled by what came from her mouth. Not sweet chirps, as the creatures sang, but hoarse, grating noises that wavered in pitch. Nevertheless, she kept trying. Over and over she forced sounds from her throat, out through her mouth, until she was satisfied by what she heard, until she too was singing to Creator, but in firm, smooth tones.

Peering to her left, to her right, up, down, woman was awestruck by the beauty that surrounded her. Trees, some with straight trunks that rose high into the heavens, others with branches reaching out like canopies. Flowers of bright red and yellow and orange, their boldness and brilliance stirring her to leap and laugh. Blossoms of pink and white and lavender, their subdued tones inspiring her to be still and smile inside.

With careful steps she began to explore this world she'd been propelled into. She followed the trail of a scent until she came upon a lavish vine stretching from bough to bough. She climbed a tree and placing her nose against the vine's small white blossoms, inhaled the spicy fragrance.

Life, it seemed, smelled good.

She came upon a gurgling stream. Seated on a large rock, the sun above warming her shoulders, Woman dipped her bare feet into water so clear she could see the pebbles beneath it. Coolness tickled her toes and sent darts of pleasure up her legs.

Life, it seemed, felt good.

She came upon a tree laden with yellow fruit. Plucking one from a branch, she bit into its soft flesh, savoring its mellowness. From a bush thick with red berries, she pulled off a cluster, put them in her mouth, and allowed the sweet juice to run down her chin.

Life, it seemed, tasted good.

Woman quickly grew accustomed to living in the wonderful garden, where luxuriant trees stretched to the sky, where everything was pleasing to the senses. She took pleasure in tilling the earth, the soil caked beneath her fingernails. She chained flowers into a necklace, stuck blossoms in her hair, rubbed berry juice onto her cheeks. She ate of the bushes and trees.

When Woman gazed into the pool of water, she recognized that she was as beautiful as the rest of Creation. She liked the width of her hips and the strong legs that supported her. She liked her round breasts. Yes, she looked at her body and saw that it was good. Wonderful, in fact.

She became acquainted with the animals with whom she shared the garden, sometimes running alongside them, at other times sitting quietly and scratching their heads. One evening Creator assigned her the task of naming the animals. For many days Woman passed among them, running her fingers through fur and feathers, playfully allowing their tongues to caress her face. She respected the power that came with naming each being and pledged never to forget that they, like she, had been formed by Creator.

Pulling from the fertile soil life-sustaining fruits and vegetables, romping with the animals, Woman felt at one with the earth. Regularly, toward the end of the day, just as the sun was about to reach the horizon, she paused to sing praises to Creator. She gave thanks for the beauty and bounty that surrounded her.

Something was missing however. The birds did not stand still long enough to carry on a conversation, the giraffe always had its head in the treetops, and the goat wasn't interested in what she was thinking.

One day Woman said to Creator, "I'm lonely." And she began to cry. Which made Creator sad also.

While Creator pondered how the problem might be solved, Woman did what she usually did to ease her mind: She tilled the garden. It was upon watching Woman, her hands burrowing in the dirt, that Creator had an idea. Taking a clump of rich soil from the earth and adding to it water from the crystal clear stream, Creator shaped the handful of soil, giving it wide hips and thick legs and breasts. Creator breathed life into this form.

A girlfriend.

Survival

Genesis 6–8

Because of humanity's wickedness, God decides to bring a flood upon the entire earth, thus destroying everything. Only Noah and his family are to be spared, along with two of every species, one male and one female. God gives Noah instructions on how to build an ark, so that when the time for the flood comes, his family and the animals are kept safe from the raging waters.

It isn't hard to imagine that such a complicated undertaking would require the organizational skills of a woman. Neither is it a stretch to relate to another time when mothers felt at odds with the violent culture and feared the devastation of the earth.

Whether Noah is female or male, whether God is father or mother, the story is troubling. What parent kills his/her own offspring? What artist destroys his/her creation?

THEY WERE corrupt times, with people using their imaginations for evil and their hands for destruction. God's creation was treated with disrespect, and in her children's hearts violence prevailed.

One woman, however, a woman named Nochat, loved and respected God's creation. She had no desire for power over others and treated all living things with reverence. As she carried out her daily tasks, she would stop to converse with the goats or sheep, with foraging mice, even with the occasional lion she met while gathering berries. Never did she fail to thank the plants she harvested for providing nourishment.

Survival

The evil times made it hard for a mother to teach her children gentleness and compassion and respect. Nevertheless, Nochat persisted, instructing her daughters and sons to honor God the Mother as she did, by respecting the earth and its bounty, by bringing harm to no living being.

As a child, Nochat had been mocked by her brothers when she cried over a dead bird or lamb. Her sisters had laughed when they witnessed her exuberance over a sunrise, light feathery clouds, a fresh blossom. Now that she was an adult, her neighbors treated her and her children with scorn. Every family needed a man, they claimed. Besides, she was a strange woman, who drew pictures in the sand and told stories that came from what they mockingly called her *deranged mind*. Strangest of all, they said, was the way Nochat and her children made friends with animals, stroking the fur of even the wildest ones, running and jumping with the fleetest.

One day, while Nochat gathered figs with her granddaughters, God called her aside. "I need to talk," God said. As the two of them walked along a dry river bed, God spoke of how deeply saddened she was by the rebelliousness of her creation. Nochat understood, for she too had witnessed the evil ways of women and men.

"I wish I'd never given birth to this world," God said. "My children no longer honor me. They conspire to seize power over each other and kill their sisters and brothers. They exploit the earth and defile its beauty. Day after day I brood over what to do." God heaved a heavy sigh. After a long silence she continued. "I—I—I—" Again God paused. "I have decided to bring a flood and let it destroy all that is on the face of the earth. Only you and your family will I save."

Nochat was dismayed by God's plan. "It's wrong," she argued, "for a loving mother, even when her children disobey, to destroy them. No matter how heart-broken you are, you must hold on to a hope they will change."

"And if there are no signs that will ever happen?" God asked.

Nochat had no answer.

In the days that followed, the two of them continued to disagree. God said it was more benevolent to take the lives of her children all at once than allow them to destroy each other slowly.

Nochat claimed that not every living thing upon the earth was depraved and that even the wicked can be taught to love. "Besides, children and plants and animals should not be punished because of others' corruption."

"A creator learns from her mistakes," God insisted. "When she sees that her work is seriously flawed, she is obligated to demolish it and begin anew."

As hard as Nochat tried, she could not change God's mind. God's only concession was that Nochat could save two of every kind of animal.

Near the horizon a large orange moon was beginning its ascent. No one paid much attention to Nochat as she rose from her place by the fire, a stick in hand, and squatted at the lighted circle's edge. After a while, one of the children came to peer over her shoulder.

"What are you drawing, Grandmother?"

"I'm not sure."

"It looks something like a boat. Only bigger."

"Yes, it does rather."

"Have you ever seen one of these, Grandmother?"

"No, God told me to draw it. An ark, she calls it."

"Whatever for?"

"We're going to need it, God says."

Her children and grandchildren gathered around Nochat, studying her outline in the dirt.

"We are going to use this picture to build a real one," she told them all. "For a great rain is coming and water will cover the earth."

Because the land was parched and many days had passed since rain had fallen, Nochat's family found her words hard to believe. Nevertheless, the following day the adults set about preparing wood and shaping pegs while the small children wove hemp for lashing. Three hundred cubits long the craft was to be, and fifty cubits wide. With many rooms and three decks. Foolish though the efforts appeared, everyone in the family worked.

Each evening neighbors came by to laugh, for they had never seen anything quite like this wooden structure that kept getting bigger and bigger. Then bigger yet.

"It looks a little like a boat," they would say.

"Yes, it does rather," one of Nochat's grandchildren would answer.

"Have you ever seen one of these?" they would ask.

"No."

"So you imagined it."

"God told our grandmother to build it."

At this point the neighbors would burst out laughing and ask each other, "How likely is it that God only speaks to this crazy woman?"

Their laughter increased when the vessel was finished, when out in the open field it stood, monstrous in size. Useless too—or so it seemed.

"Next," Nochat told her children and grandchildren, "we will collect animals, two of each kind, male and female." So they went forth to gather antelopes and pigeons, oryx and quails. And every other beast of the field and bird of the air.

Now, only seven days had passed since the construction of the craft had been completed, and the animals were barely settled in their stalls. Nochat looked into the west and saw a great storm cloud gathering. "It is time," she said. Scurrying her family aboard the ark, she closed the doors.

What started as a gentle pitter-patter turned into hammering rain, causing the parched land to become moist at first, then saturated. Narrow streams became roaring rivers. Then rivers merged to form one vast sea, which lifted the ark from the land and set it afloat. Upon the waves of the sea, the vessel rolled and pitched, sometimes listing to one side so that animals and people tumbled to the floor, landing on top of one another, nearly suffocating those on the bottom of the pile.

Each night Nochat lay on the floor of the rocking vessel, worrying about her cousins and sisters-in-law, about their children and the plants and animals. About her neighbors even, though they'd always been unkind. Perhaps she should not have followed God's directions so closely but built a bigger ark that could have held more people. Or she ought to have shared the detailed instructions with others so they might have built their own. Eventually she would fall asleep to the sounds of the rain pounding against the roof and of the creaking vessel as it strained to stay afloat.

How many days had it been now? Ten? Twenty? The grandchildren, who at first explored every nook and occupied themselves by playing with the animals, had become restless. They'd lost interest in Nochat's stories and groaned whenever she posed a riddle.

"When can we go outside and play?" they asked time and again, tugging at her garments, wrapping their arms around her legs.

"There's nothing to do," one would whine, her chorus soon taken up by the others.

They scrapped among themselves, chasing each other, hitting and kicking. Yelling and screaming so loudly that their parents could not help but grab them at times and demand their silence. Not that the adults were behaving any better. Much as they had done as children, they bickered among themselves then appealed to Nochat to intervene.

It was easier to love her family on land, she decided, where adults could scatter and children had room to play their games. It was easier to love the animals when their excrement was not her concern. She who enjoyed nothing more than walking alongside a chirping rivulet was now surrounded by the clamor of shrieking children, the din of animals barking or mewing or roaring or whinnying. After a while their noises, their complaints, their demands became like the rain—incessant—and she wanted to flee. But there was no place to escape to.

On the thirtieth day, when the rains weren't pounding quite as hard and the ark wasn't rocking so violently, Nochat was able to step out onto the deck. Holding firmly to the rail, she looked with despair at what was before her. The gray of sky met the gray of water, and in every direction there was no sign of life. What was familiar had been submerged so that there were no landmarks, and she had no idea where she was or where she was going.

"How can you say you love me," she yelled out at God, "when you have destroyed nearly everything I hold dear? The olive trees with their gnarled branches and fragrant white buds, the handsome wolves who came to be petted, the paths that wound along rugged hillsides and down into the beautiful fertile valley."

God did not answer.

One morning Nochat and her children and her grandchildren awoke to a strange sound—rather to its absence. The rain had stopped. The animals too noticed, for their din ceased, as if they were waiting for a signal about what to do next. That was the first indication—the silence—that this day would be different. The second was the bright sunlight splattering the ark.

For days the family gazed out from the deck, waiting for the waters to recede. Where were they, they kept asking each other.

All was still calm the afternoon everyone stood around Nochat as she lifted a dove. "Go find land," she instructed it. But it soon returned, bringing no sign that land was emerging from the water's shroud. Seven days later Nochat again released the dove. This time it did not return right away.

"She tried too hard," one of Nochat's sons said, "flying and flying, until finally her wings gave out and she plunged into the water."

"She's lost," a granddaughter suggested, "and is flying around and around."

It was the oldest grandchild who first called out, "Look, look, there she is!" In her beak the dove carried an olive branch.

That day Nochat and her family felt the rebirth of hope, so that even though they did not know when they would again step on firm ground, they were not despondent as they waited.

Once the waters had receded and puddles of every dimension dotted the earth, Nochat went from the ark, she and her children and grandchildren. And every pair of animals: the ferrets and gazelles, the ibex and asps, all left the ark.

When every animal had crept or leaped or flown to the north, the south, the east, the west, Nochat looked at the desolation around her and felt a great emptiness. Nothing she had known remained. She sat upon the ground and cried.

"What kind of mother are you," she called out to God, "that you would strangle your own child because it is willful? What kind of God are you that you would create animals as lovely as gazelles, as clever as foxes, as playful as goats, then kill them? What kind of God creates beautiful trees and flowers then destroys them?"

From nearby came the faint sound of weeping. The weeping became loud sobs. Then a haunting keen pierced the stillness of the desolate landscape.

"What have I done?" Nochat heard God wail. "What have I done?" Nochat rose and approached the Creator. Put her arms around God. Let God cry against her breast. "In the beginning I had such hopes and dreams, imagining everything to stay as lovely as it was. But my children spurned my love, and when I gazed upon all I had created, I decided it no longer had any value. I convinced myself that my rebellious children deserved my wrath."

Survival

She said nothing for a while, simply sat there nestled in Nochat's arms, heaving sobs of an immenseness that only God can heave.

"It is as if I have cut off my own breast," she cried out, "plunged a knife into my own heart. To destroy what I had created was to destroy part of myself."

For days the two remained in that place, God speaking of her regrets over the devastation she had wrought, Nochat lamenting the loss of the people and animals she had loved.

One afternoon God hiccoughed and stood. "My mourning will never cease, but it is time for me to set about recreating. First, though, I will make a promise, Nochet. I promise you and your descendents and every living creature that has come to this place on the ark—I promise that I will never again release the waters to destroy the earth by flood."

As God spoke, she spread an immense arc of colors across the sky. Lavender, red, blue, and yellow, it was, with a span so wide that its ends could not be seen. "This is a sign of my covenant. You will never again need to fear my wrath."

With heavy heart Nochat went to get the family's mildewed garments out of the ark so that she might spread them in the sun.

With heavy heart God set about rebuilding the earth.

Confused

Genesis 11:1–9

Humankind shares a common language—until a group decides to build a great city and a great tower, an action God views as arrogant. God decides to confuse their communication. The story of the Tower of Babel has sometimes been used to explain why the earth is inhabited by people who speak different languages.

Women, too, once spoke a common language.

THERE WAS a time when women understood each other, for sorrow was the language that connected them. Some held the hands of sisters and friends as they died at childbirth. Many wept at the graves of their children taken by disease or hunger. Those who did not lose sisters or friends or children still grasped the horror and mourned with women who did.

Wars claimed the lives of husbands, brothers, sons. Women's homes were invaded, their bodies raped. Those who did not witness war still grasped its horror and mourned with women who did.

Yes, it used to be that women everywhere understood the language of sorrow.

Then some migrated, found a place to the west. There they said to one another, "Come, let us build ourselves a great city, and towers that extend to the heavens, and let us make a name for ourselves so that our wealth will be recognized over all the earth."

When they had built the city and the towers, the women said among themselves, "See what great feats we are able to do."

But God looked down upon the city and its towers and said, "Look, those women have built this grand city and think they have made a name for themselves. But they have forgotten the language of sorrow that used to connect them to others. They are too intent upon accumulating wealth to recognize the suffering of those in distant lands who lose sisters and friends at childbirth. They are too busy to pay attention to the agony of women in distant lands who weep at the graves of children who have died of disease or hunger. They no longer listen to the voices of women whose homes are invaded, their bodies raped when war spreads over their land."

So God turned from the women who had built a city and towers that reached the heavens, choosing instead to accompany those who lived with sadness and oppression. God named the city with the tall towers Babel, which means *confused*. Because the women who lived there no longer understood what mattered in God's sight.

Not All Who Wander are Lost

Genesis 12–22

"Leave your country," God tells Abraham, "and go to the land I will show you." God promises to bless Abraham and "make of you a great nation." Accompanied by Sarah, his wife, and Lot, his nephew, Abraham heads for Canaan. Herdsmen, he and Lot move their flocks from place to place, even traveling as far as Egypt during a time of famine. Eventually, because the size of their herds has increased and their shepherds compete for grazing space, the two men part ways.

Female Abrahams, too, follow God's call to leave the familiar and head for a far-away destination. The journey is not without hardship and loneliness, times when these daring women consider turning back. Yet God's presence gives them courage.

Muslims, Jews, and Christians trace their ancestry back to Abraham.

EVEN AS a child I was restless, often escaping the light around the evening fire to venture into the darkness. Farther and farther I wandered, during the day and after dark, until I was familiar with every knoll and dip in the surrounding landscape. With my eyes closed I could see what the sun looked like as it rose over the lands to the east and set behind the hills to the west.

What was on the other side of the river, I wondered. Beyond the distant hills? I also entertained questions about God Most High. Did she reside beyond the mountains? In the cities? I dreamed of exploring faraway places.

---

* I am grateful to the work of Elie Wiesel in "The Sacrifice of Isaac: A Survivor's Story," in *Messengers of God* (New York: Simon and Shuster, 1976).

My father assured me that I would find nothing different or interesting beyond the river. Besides, it was not appropriate for a young woman to journey forth, he insisted. Or to search for God Most High. Whether God Most High could be found beyond the mountains or in the city was not important; what mattered was that she dwelt with *us*.

His simple answers made me even more impatient to journey afar. I became convinced that my homeland was no place for one like me. A curious woman. A woman who sought adventure.

For generations the God of my people has been God Most High, the one who stirs the heavens and earth, who destroys and rescues. Like others, my husband and I made sacrifices to her out of fear. Yet questions kept coming to me: If she was to be feared, why did her creation fill me with so much pleasure? The peaceful stream I took clear water from. The soft fox kit I held.

It is as if it happened in another lifetime, that day long ago when she first came to me. I had just started to explore a shallow cave when I heard a voice: "We are alike, you know." Instinctively I knew it was the voice of God Most High. "Who but an adventuresome God would have created contradiction?" she asked. "Henna and thistle, for example. The poisonous berry and sweet date. The booming shout of a man and the gentle song of a mother with her infant."

"I have often considered the rose and the thorn," I said. "The playful cub that becomes a fierce lion. Why did you create animals so that they must eat each other to survive? Why did you create a world with the serene beauty of a meadow, yet also the storm and earthquake?" I had scores of questions.

After we'd engaged in a lengthy discussion, God Most High told me, "You do not belong among people who have answers but no questions. I have a better place for you, a place where you can flourish, where your intelligence will serve you well."

My intelligence? No one else had ever said I was intelligent.

"In that place I will make of your offspring a great nation, so that you will be a blessing to all."

A new land, a place where I could flourish, she promised. A place where I would not be considered a nuisance, a woman with too many questions. A new role: mother, grandmother, ancestor.

As exciting as her invitation sounded, as much as I wanted to follow the path she had prepared for me, I could not easily separate myself from my people. Voices within said I should stay with them, try to be the woman my parents and husband wanted me to be: committed to kin, contented with the life I had. To embark on a journey would be leaving familiar customs and language. Memories, too, many of them pleasant.

Leaving all to follow the God I knew mainly through tradition. What if after forsaking all security I ended up in a faraway land and did *not* flourish, did *not* become a blessing to all? But if I stayed my spirit would surely die. I decided to go.

"Why do you want to go away," my husband asked, "when everything you need is right here?"

"It will be dangerous," my mother and aunts said.

Cousins tried to convince me that beyond my familiar homeland there was nothing better than what I already had. I heard whispers, barely within earshot, predicting that as soon as hardship came I'd be back. Only my oldest sister remained quiet.

At night everyone's warnings invaded my dreams. I was lost; strangers lifted their hands against me. Yet when morning dawned, though I had no more assurance than I'd had the night before, I would again trust God Most High's promise to remain with me. To bless me.

There were of course arguments with my husband. If the husband said stay, the wife should stay, he lectured. It was a woman's duty to obey. I insisted that a woman must follow the call of God Most High. Finally, reluctantly, my husband agreed to accompany me. My favorite niece too, my middle sister's oldest daughter, who had started to dream about her own future.

We had no trouble deciding what to take, what to leave behind, for our possessions were few. Nearly everything we planned to carry was essential for survival: foodstuffs, utensils, medicinal herbs, several goats and sheep.

The evening before we were to leave, my oldest sister drew me aside and handed me what I recognized as her favorite bracelet. "Take this with you," she said, tears in her eyes, "so that a part of me ventures out too."

It had not occurred to me that she might also want to make the journey. Her foot had been crushed by a ewe when she'd been but a baby, and as the oldest daughter she was expected to care for our parents. I had assumed she was content to stay.

As I put the bracelet on my arm, I recognized that my journey would be for her as well.

Ah, I remember the day of departure as if it were yesterday. Of course I cried—from fear or relief or sorrow, I do not know—as our small caravan set out in the faint light of early morning. I led the way, on foot, my head held high, my gaze fixed on the distant horizon.

Since God Most High had promised to bless me, I assumed our travels would be without hardship and danger. And indeed the journey was easy at first. Each new vista delighted me and inspired me to keep moving forward.

But I discovered that while I sometimes journeyed in the protective shadow of God Most High, at other times she remained beyond my reach. Each time, upon her reappearance I built an altar, partly to honor and thank her for returning, partly to serve as a future meeting place for the two of us.

Many nights I would throw a blanket over my shoulders and step out of the tent. The nights were cold and clear, with stars so brilliant I felt as if I could reach up and pluck some from the sky. Only my husband's snores and the faint sounds of restless animals broke the stark mantel of silence. Seated upon a large rock or on the ground, I spoke with God Most High. Rather she spoke to me, reminding me over and over that I was intelligent and capable and lovely, for I still did not always believe her affirming words.

Gradually, as I began to accept my worthiness, our encounters changed. God Most High asked what I had been thinking, laughed at my jokes, praised my ingenuity. I too listened as she spoke of loneliness, for many had forsaken my dear friend and turned to other gods. In those moments of honesty I discovered what a true companion I had gained. Not only one who accompanied me on the arduous journey, inspiring me to go forward and not be afraid, but one who understood me better than I understood myself.

There were times too, when for hours the two of us argued, each defending a position, neither willing to acquiesce. Whether evil should be punished, for example. They were pleasurable too, the disagreements, for my friend valued a woman who spoke her mind, and I enjoyed the mental challenges.

"How can I truly know you?" I asked one night.

"Knowing me," she said, "will take a lifetime."

I was disappointed, but as our caravan journeyed the following day, I considered her response. Ah, I finally saw: her nature was not a mystery to be solved; on the contrary it opened to questions without answers. Then to more questions. The quest to fathom her nature was for a mind that relished searching but was content not to find. A mind like mine, for I had no wish to build a prison of knowledge around her.

To find the place where she belongs, where she will flourish, a woman sometimes has to change directions several times. Meanwhile, God Most High is attending to other business. More than once I found myself in rugged terrain, making slow and laborious progress.

There was a period when many days passed without any sign of God Most High. One day our caravan would be battered by the harshness of the sun, the next by the ferocity of the wind.

"I should have known better than to follow a woman," my husband complained.

I had assumed I could handle hardship. After all, I had planned well. Besides, God Most High had said I was an intelligent woman. But now the dry earth I trod became the parched soil of my soul, and I knew that nothing could grow there. It was unexpected, this sense of desolation. Scanning the landscape, I saw nothing that made me hopeful. I questioned the wisdom of having left security behind and began to doubt God Most High's lofty promises.

When would I find the place where I could flourish? How would a great nation come of me if I had no children? A blessing to all? Hardly.

At those times of hopelessness, I often glanced down and saw my sister's bracelet on my wrist. I reminded myself that she would rejoice if she had legs strong enough to be making this journey. Her ongoing determination to survive sustained me. She, more than anyone, would be disappointed if I returned home.

It's part of the journey, I discovered: enduring times of emptiness and discouragement as well as those of satisfaction.

"But you have brought us back to Bethel," I complained to God Most High. We had traveled in a circle.

"This is the in-between place, not the final destination," she assured me.

At Bethel my niece and I prospered, accumulating gold and silver, numerous flocks and herds, too. As we discussed our achievements one evening, arrogantly asserting as we often did that success comes to those who risk, I noticed that I was sliding my sister's bracelet up and down my arm. It occurred to me that she did not have the freedom to risk. Her injured body and loyalty to our parents bound her to one place so that she would never have my wealth.

Until that moment I had simply accepted God Most High's explanations for why I was chosen, her words about my intellect and adventuresome spirit pleasing to my ear. Yet my equally intelligent sister yearned for adventure and success too. How, I wondered, can a woman feel blessed if her sister has no similar opportunities?

I had been assuming that my wealth was the blessing God Most High had spoken of. That night in the tent, next to my husband, I lay awake considering the rest of God Most High's promise: "So that you will be a blessing to all." Instead of being a blessing to all, I was putting my energy into gaining wealth and guarding my possessions. I was using my riches to gain stature and power. I had ceased marveling over the earth's glories and lost my curiosity.

In the days that followed, the restlessness returned. What was beyond the mountains? The prospect of newness again excited me. New people, new landscapes. New opportunities to become a blessing for others rather than a woman whose primary goal was to accumulate.

My husband whined that life was good in Bethel; it made no sense to leave. My niece said she was ready to move on too. We decided to go in separate directions, though. She chose the plain; my husband and I headed toward the mountains.

I awoke from a deep sleep, seized by terror. I had no idea what the source of my anxiety was, only a feeling of deep, deep dread.

I called out to God Most High.

An abyss of silence came back to me. Dark, empty silence.

I sensed her approach. Yet she said nothing.

"Speak to me," I shouted. "Tell me, why do I feel this way?"

I was trembling by now. Though awake, I began to picture, as in a dream, a most wretched scene. Rows and rows of people, their heads lowered as they walked, walked, into a powerful wind. I could not see their faces, yet I recognized in the slump of their shoulders, the slow plodding, their sense of desolation, their lack of hope.

Overcome by sorrow, I began to weep. "What does it mean? What does it mean?" I begged to know.

In her answer I heard a sadness yet greater than my own, one that seemed to pierce the very being of God Most High. "You are looking into the future with me. These are your descendents. They will be sojourners in a land that is not theirs and will be slaves, oppressed for four hundred years."

"Then this journey is in vain," I cried out. "Why should I struggle to find a place that offers heartache?"

"Because I am always creating. Even when my desire for harmony is obstructed I will be their God. I will comfort them. Leave the future to me."

I have lived my full span of years. I have buried my husband in the cave where I too will be laid to rest.

The journey was long and arduous, but eventually I arrived in this land, where I did indeed flourish. I have been blessed with children and grandchildren who admire the harmony of God Most High's creation and praise her for it. They too are restless and full of questions. I have taught them that God Most High is a God of mystery and that while she delights in their efforts to understand her, she cannot be contained.

I remain a woman of wealth, but being blessed is less tangible than silver and gold. It is in seeing my heirs come to trust God Most High, in having my neighbors regard me as a woman of integrity and wisdom.

The journey itself was part of the blessing. I have been allowed to see what's beyond the next mountain, on the other side of the river. The times that have been arid or fraught with dangers—they have been part of the blessing too, for I have survived them. A woman learns from such times. She learns that she is strong and capable. Such knowledge is certainly a blessing.

I have had the opportunity to be not just a wanderer over land but a wanderer in my mind as well. Since my youth I have explored the mysteries of God Most High. Sometimes I have been allowed to spend time in her shadow; at other times I have walked and walked but she has been beyond my reach. The times with her, those spent searching for her too, have been a blessing.

Has my name become great? That is for future generations to decide. If it is to be, the greatness will be the result of putting myself in new situations, facing the challenges, taking actions that will provide a better place for my neighbors and descendents.

I still think of my oldest sister. I do not know whether she still breathes. I assume she lived out her days as our mother and her mother and our grandmother's mother lived theirs. Several times I have challenged God Most High's intentions. Why should I have flourished while my sister had no similar opportunities?

If I could see her again, what would I tell her? Not how grateful I am that God Most High chose me. No, that would be wrong. I would hold my sister close and express gratitude for her hard work. Her sacrifice allowed me to leave our parents and venture forth. I would assure her that the blessings of God Most High were not mine alone. They were also for future generations, for our parents' grandchildren and those who come after them.

The Lamb that Was Slain

Genesis 22

"Take your son, and go to the land of Moriah, and offer him there as a burnt offering," God tells Abraham. Abraham follows God's instructions until, at the last minute, an angel intervenes, telling Abraham not to lay his hand upon the boy.

Seeing Isaac as female reminds us of young girls who are victims of violence and abuse.

It is late at night, but I lie with my eyes wide open, too excited to sleep. As soon as day breaks I get to go with Father up to the mountains. To make a sacrifice. It is a long trip, he says, it will take several days. I've been such a good girl that I get to go with him. Mother will pack food for us to take along and two servants will go too, and we'll see animals. Because I've been a good girl. I've been a good girl and Father loves me.

Everybody respects him. He tells them how to make sacrifices and how God wants to be worshipped. They call him Leader, and they tell each other he is a man of God.

I wish I could go to sleep. I shall just lie here and try not to think about anything. Make my mind blank. Not think about anything.

I like being the daughter of an important man, I like standing near him while he speaks to the people. God is with you in all that you do, I heard a man tell him once.

It must be nearly morning, but I have not been able to sleep at all, I am so excited. Mother does not want me to go. She said it

HAD EVE COME FIRST AND JONAH BEEN A WOMAN

is too long a trip for a child, but Father said I am hardly a child any more, I am almost a woman. He winked at me when he said it, because we all know I am not really almost a woman.

Get a good night's sleep, Father told me before I went to bed. I am trying hard to do what he said.

I hear people moving around. It is still dark but the servants are getting everything ready, and I hear Father telling them what to do. Telling them what food to pack for our trip.

I am going to get up.

Mother sets bread and goat cheese in front of me, but I push the food away. I want us to be on our way. I want to help Father make the sacrifice.

It is barely daylight when we leave for the mountain. I sit on the donkey in front of him. I do not fear falling off while our bodies bounce up and down, because he has wrapped his arms around me. I know he will not let anything bad happen to me. We talk as we ride, and he makes jokes, which I laugh at. Then I make jokes too, and he laughs. Behind us two servants carry our provisions. And the wood for the sacrifice.

I am sleepy. With Father's arms wrapped around me, while we bounce up and down, I fall asleep.

Father says I am a good little traveler. I will do anything to make him happy, that is why I do not ask, Are we almost there? That is why I do not tell him that my bottom is getting sore from bouncing around on the donkey. So I am glad he says that—that I am a good little traveler.

See way over there? he asks. He is pointing to a mountain far away. That is where we are going, just you and me, nobody else. What about the servants, I want to know, and he says they are going to stay here while we go up there, just the two of us.

And I love Father for letting me go way up there with him. Just the two of us, Father and me.

The Lamb that Was Slain

Stay here with the donkey, he tells the servants. My daughter and I will go yonder and come again to you.

He puts a bundle of wood on my shoulders. It is very heavy, but it is an honor to help with the sacrifice, so I carry the wood without complaining, the same way I have traveled without complaining. We begin the walk up to the high place.

I am tired, but Father keeps telling me that it's only a little farther. So I do not complain. No, a good girl never complains.

This is the place, my father says after we have been climbing a long time. But I have a question. We have the fire and the wood, but where is the lamb for the offering? He tells me God will give us a lamb for the burnt offering. I do not understand.

He wants me to lie down on the bed of rocks he has prepared, but I do not want to. Something is wrong, why does he want me to lie down? It is not night time yet.

I start to cry. I brought you up here because you are a big girl, he says. So I try not to cry and I wipe my nose on my arm. This will not hurt, he tells me. What won't hurt? Something is wrong, but I do not know what. I cannot call out for help, because the two servants are far away. Besides, Father says it all has to do with my being a big girl now.

I do not like the look in his eyes.

I am to be the sacrifice. I understand now, I am to be the sacrifice. My father is crying. God told me to do this, he says. And he knows what God wants, because I heard a man tell him, God is with you in all that you do. And I know that I am supposed to obey him, even when he tells me to lie down on the rocks.

They hurt my back. I cry out but Father says, Sshh, it is all right, this is what God wants.

God wants me to hurt this way? I think I am going to die. But Father does not like it when I complain. I know what I will do, I will not let myself feel anything. I will not let it hurt. I'll never let anything hurt again. I do not feel any pain. I will never let anything hurt again.

Why did Father bring me to this faraway place where I cannot call out for anyone to help me?

I am the sacrifice. Father and God have chosen me. I am father's little girl and he and God have chosen me to be the sacrifice. So I will not cry out, I will not complain that the rocks hurt my back, that the rope hurts my hands.

Do not tell anybody what happened up there. You are a big girl now, and you can keep a secret.

God is with you in all that you do, I heard a man tell Father.

Insubordination

Genesis 22

"Take your son, and go to the land of Moriah, and offer him there as a burnt offering," God tells Abraham. Abraham follows God's instructions until, at the last minute, an angel intervenes, telling Abraham not to lay his hand upon the boy.

How might a mother respond?

WHEN SHE observed the boy practicing his skills at bow and arrow in the nearby field, she realized he'd grown as tall as the tree from which she was gathering figs. A handsome boy he was, a man almost, with wide shoulders and laughing eyes. What mother would not look upon such a son with love and delight?

His father accused her of being overprotective, made fun of her fears. "How will he grow to be a man if you don't let him out of your sight?" he asked.

How could she explain her attachment? Yes, he'd been born in her later years, well past the time when most women bear children. Certainly she was moved by his innocent face that daily turned to her with trust and devotion. She, perhaps more than anyone, recognized that his agile mind and physical prowess would lead to eventual power and influence.

But her affection was due to more than that. "You will be the ancestor of a multitude of nations," God had promised her. Who but this precious son would provide the heirs? The future rested on the boy. He was her hope.

Knife in hand, Abrama held the goat firmly to the ground. Its flesh would provide the evening meal for family and servants. Just as she put the knife to its neck, the goat wiggled out from beneath her and scurried off. Chasing after it, Abrama stumbled and fell to the ground, her garments tangled between her legs.

It was at this importune moment that the voice of God called out, "Abrama."

"Catch that goat!" she yelled to one of the servants, at the same time standing and brushing the dust from her clothes. She walked away from the compound toward the cedar grove where she and her God often met.

God made no introductory remarks, as a friend might, no comment about the wiliness of goats or inquiry about the aching shoulder that had lately been plaguing Abrama.

"Take your son, your only son, Isaac, whom you love, and go down to the land of Moriah."

Abrama crossed her arms. "For what purpose?"

"My command is not for you to question."

"Well, if I'm going to make such a long trip, I want to know its purpose."

"You are to offer him as a burnt offering on one of the mountains that I shall show you."

Abrama assumed old age interfered with her hearing. Eyebrows knit, she put her hand to her ear. "Say that again?"

"Take Isaac, the son whom you love, and go down to the land of Moriah and place him upon the altar as a sacrifice."

"But the heathens do that. They place virgins and young men upon altars of fire. You do not ask for such sacrifices."

"Do as I say," God's voice boomed.

Abrama stood planted, feet apart, hands on hips. "You're asking me to kill my own son? You promised I would be the mother of nations, that through me the nations of the earth will be blessed. I demand to know why you are asking this of me."

"Do not question me. It is enough that I tell you to do it."

"Am I to obey you even when you command me to perform an act that goes counter to the ways you have taught me?"

"That is right."

"Well, I refuse." And she stomped away.

"That's the problem with old women," God muttered. "They no longer accept authority."

Jabbok Night

Genesis 27–32

After Jacob cheats his brother Esau out of their father's blessing, he journeys to another land to find a wife. This time he is the one cheated, given a different woman than the one he wanted to marry. Years later, as he is about to return to the land of his kindred, along the bank of the Jabbok River, Jacob wrestles with a mysterious being. God? An Angel? His own conscience?

Women too have lied and betrayed the trust of another. Many are alienated from a sister or brother, a former friend. Whom do they confront nights, along the river?

ALONE. I'M alone. Only a short time earlier the noises of goats, sheep, camels, and cows surrounded me. Not to mention the constant "if you want my opinion" remarks of the men and all the commotion that eleven children can generate. The livestock, the men, the children, and the maids—in the dark of night I sent all of them across the ford of the Jabbok.

I'm impressed with my own resourcefulness. If the gifts fail to adequately impress Essa, at least my possessions will be safe from her revenge.

They do not arise out of a sense of guilt, the gifts. After all, lying was my mother's idea, and events evolved without my doing much. "Upon me be your curse, my daughter," Mother said, holding forth the savory game she'd prepared. Then, wrapping my sister's coat around me, she gave me a quick kiss and pushed me toward my father.

Jabbok Night

It's your fault, Mother. The shadows of the womb made me accustomed to darkness. Besides, *you* were the one who schemed so that I might have Daddy's blessing. Secrecy and deceit originated in *your* mind, not in mine.

Still I must admit perverse pleasure in successfully deceiving someone. "Here I am, Father. Here's your daughter, Essa," I said. "Eat of my game, that you may bless me." And he was ignorant enough—or trusting enough—to believe me. When he heard my voice, touched the kid skins Mother had placed on my hands, even smelled me, he couldn't tell the difference. A father, even a blind one who can't tell the difference between his daughters, deserves to be fooled. Besides, who, if the opportunity to be blessed arose, would refuse it?

Tomorrow, for the first time in many years, my sister and I will face each other, explore each others' eyes for some reason to—.

Face. If father had been able to see my face, all this would never have happened. Foolish man, to have fallen for the kids'-skin-on-the-arms trick. Foolish sister. Anyone that stupid should have neither the birthright nor Daddy's blessing. No, it's not fair to either of them. Or to my mother. I'm blaming all of them for my own chicanery. The deceiver, not the deceived, deserves the scorn.

The messengers say Essa is approaching. She has no reason to trust the sister who tricked her. I have no reason to believe the two of us can merely come together face-to-face as if the past does not exist.

Face. What will hers look like after all these years? What does my own look like? Certainly weathered from hot, dry days in the sun. Certainly wiser.

Wise from dealing with Laban. When morning came, in the diffused light that seeped into the tent, I looked into a face bearing no resemblance to the son he'd promised me. I awoke to discover I had committed myself to an energetic youth but got instead his

31

brother, dull and lethargic; and instead of intimacy and vulnerability, I was in a relationship characterized by distance and self-protection. I had given passions of the night to one weak of vision and weak in spirit.

What were my options? I could have closed my eyes, continued the illusion of the night, convinced myself that I was satisfied. Or I could leave the tent in search of one who satisfied my desires. Put my energies into getting what I deserved.

In spite of having been tricked, I was expected to feel gratitude, gratitude that my needs were taken care of. Why, how blessed I was just to be part of Laban's clan.

The community held me up as a paradigm, said the family couldn't function without me. All of this a ruse to keep me working harder than anyone else. Rewards dangled in front of me. Just seven years for this one. Then it was seven more.

For how many years—I've lost track—I worked and worked, always for someone else, never for myself. It's because of my managerial abilities, my frugality, the strain of my back from early morning to late at night, that Laban became wealthy. If it weren't for me his place would be a bowl of dust with a few scraggly creatures wandering around. Who's bothered to thank me? Where is my reward?

A curse on Laban. A curse on the whole community that gives legitimacy to his kind of manipulation.

But I am clever, more clever than he, that's for sure. I was able to take many more speckled sheep and goats than he ever dreamed I could find.

Oh yes, the woman Essa will meet is certainly a wiser woman.

Alone. I'm alone here on this side of the Jabbok. Alone in the darkness. Without warning, an amorphous shadow approaches. How could it exist apart from light?

Angel, God, Satan, human. Who are you? Come out of the darkness. Reveal yourself that I may know who you are. Just as the darkness protects you, it also protects me. In fact, darkness has always been my ally, and secrecy has fed my strength.

It is that power that will finally consume me, isn't it? God—if you are God—can't the same be said of you? What you love has become a part of yourself. When in the darkness you lash out at the obstacle to your plan for light and justice, you will find that unleashed, your destructive power will also destroy you.

Admittedly, not all of my goals have been worthy ones. Convinced that honesty would be ineffective, I've been dishonest. Believing my needs were for the good of all, I've secretly maneuvered to get them met and convinced myself that others benefit as much as I. All the while somehow managing to see myself as the victim, when the truth is, I am the perpetrator. Having become accustomed to the darkness, I've been unable to work in the light.

They seemed such small things—cheating my sister of a birthright and of a blessing, tricking my father-in-law out of a few animals. How is it that those events could affect me for a lifetime?

I keep asking you questions, but in response I only get more questions.

Whoever you are, you've engaged me in this contest. But I am amazingly strong. Or was it I who assailed you? In either case, I won't allow you victory. Such life-death struggles are not for the faint-hearted, you are about to see.

Is it my fault that I have lived with this restlessness? Is it my fault, Mother, that even within the darkness of your womb, before my awareness, I struggled with my sister? Surely I can't be held responsible for being stronger and shrewder than others. Should I have meekly accepted the rules everyone else lives by? Can I be blamed for going after what's due me?

If the rest of my life is to be lived in darkness, in deception, then I will remain here for the duration of the night and engage this foe with every fiber of my being.

Against the background murmur of the sluggish Jabbok, with the silence of the desert absorbing the sound of body grasping body, mind clinching mind, my scream pierces the night. Merely by touching the hollow of my thigh, the stranger has put it out of joint.

Until now I was winning. Muscles taut, nerves tensed, teeth clenched, my body was impervious to the strain, my mind impenetrable. Perhaps I only imagined I was winning, for if touch alone has brought such agony, what might have happened had my competitor exerted her full strength?

God, if it is you, why are you inflicting such pain? You are the God of comfort, of repose. Don't make me suffer this way. Let me live as I was, satisfied and guilt-free. Not this pain, God. Please, no more.

Quit now before defeat, I tell myself. Just break free, step back, command the stranger to go away. No, to quit is the greatest defeat. To quit is to choose the small world of the womb, to remain forever in its darkness. It is within the darkness of the womb that secrets and deceits, unexposed to the truths of the world outside, are nurtured.

I've always believed evil had some mystic strength. Can it be, instead, that evil is born of weakness? Is it from my weakness, not my great strength, that I've created victims?

Oh, my opponent has wounded me. But I refuse to release the hold I have.

Mind and body. Body and mind. Both feel contorted, violently twisted by the long struggle. Despite the cool, dry desert night, sweat covers me. Or is it my mind that is too slippery for the opponent to hold firm? My breath comes in heaves, shallow inhalations that cannot fill my lungs, gasps for air that seems not to be there.

Determined to be the victor—or are there victors in encounters such as this?—I demand more of my body than I've ever thought possible. How long can a person place such exigency upon it? I cannot stop now, for the moment of exhilaration still eludes me.

Here by the banks of the Jabbok, with a strength I never knew I possessed, I continue to wrestle with the stranger. On a barren landscape where there are no hiding places, I persevere.

"Let me go, for the day is breaking," my adversary pleads, apparently as afraid of daylight as I. The light is certain to expose the truth of who we both are.

By disengaging, would I let go of my opponent or would I be freeing myself? In such a clinch, who releases whom? Since I've been asked to let go it would appear that I am in the stronger position. Why then do I bear the wound, why do I feel such pain?

If she too fears the light of day, perhaps I can best her by holding on. Yet I have the feeling that if I hold fast, whatever my arms encase will vanish. In the light I will discover that I cling to nothingness.

"Let me go, for the day is breaking," she repeats. At this point I honestly don't know whether daybreak is to be feared or looked forward to. Perhaps the many questions of the night will be answered by the light of day. But perhaps there will only be more questions.

Still I have not released the stranger. She intruded into my world, not I into hers. Let her drop her own hands if she wants to end the struggle.

My sprained thigh continues to send agonizing messages to the rest of my body. I want to fall to the ground, clasp my wound, rock my body, and cry out so that the sand, the rocks, and the river hear my pain.

But I cannot simply let go and walk away. Stripped of all illusion of who I am, I'll be left with nothing but a wound. I need something to take with me, something that can transcend the pain, a reminder that an event of significance has happened at this time and in this place.

"I will not let you go unless you bless me," I shout.

Please, give our encounter legitimacy is what I'm asking. Place some benediction upon what has happened during this long night by the Jabbok, that I may carry not only pain but also power—rightful power—with me for as long as I live. Give me your blessing, that I may also remember the exultation of having totally engaged myself with another.

"What is your name?" my adversary asks.

Who are you, *really*, is what she wants to know. Clearly, she entered this encounter not knowing who she was engaging. Perhaps it would be just a game, a casual wrestle in a quiet, remote place. She probably assumed no one would get hurt. After all, I presented myself as a strong person, one who would depart unscathed. Furthermore, she was confident in her ability to protect herself from me. She got more than she bargained for, that's for sure.

What is my name? Until now it's had little meaning. I have simply lived with the name my parents gave me at birth. Before I had separateness from my mother's breast or from my father's protection, before they had any understanding of who I would be, they gave me a name, an identity. A presumptuous act, it is. How can you give to someone who is still part of you a name of her own?

If I tell my name, if I tell her who this person is who has spent such a God-awful night in combat with her, I am giving her power over me, am I not?

It's too late to fear that. Though she does not know my name, she has witnessed my most primitive emotions—my love, my hate, my pain, my guilt. She will walk away with knowledge of the deepest part of my soul.

I whisper my name.

It is outdated; it doesn't fit me anymore. There's some sadness in that realization, for I am not the person I was before this night.

With the old name I could convince myself that my motives were honorable, that despite some of my questionable deeds, I was a good woman. Tonight I stepped away from the illusions that made my life comfortable, the denial that veiled disappointment and anger.

A new name the stranger gives me: "Because you have prevailed."

If I have prevailed, why don't I feel victorious? Why do I want to curl up and whimper in the desert dawn?

Yet I am confident that someday the pain will lessen. Then I will whoop in triumph.

When Sisters Dream*

Genesis 37–46

Not only do Joseph's brothers resent his being their father's favorite, they grow tired of listening to his self-promoting dreams. Instead of killing him, which they have seriously considered, they sell him into slavery then tell their father, Jacob, that he's been killed by a wild beast. Years later, when a famine descends upon their land, the brothers travel to Egypt in search of food. There they come upon Joseph, now the governor in charge of distributing food. Later, after their father dies, the brothers ask for Joseph's forgiveness. Joseph's reply is that only God can forgive.

Women too have betrayed their sisters, even sold them into slavery. Those who have been betrayed are the ones to decide when, if ever, to forgive.

AROUND THE well, in the grazing areas, none of us spoke of what had happened. It was as if she'd never lived.

But I had dreams. Not the kind she once had, but terrifying ones where her blood cried out and demanded revenge. Like it or not, I discovered, she was still bound to us by blood.

Did my sisters have dreams like mine? I dared not ask, for not only did we never mention Josepha, we no longer discussed visions of the night. Because the two were so closely connected, Josepha and dreams.

---

* This story has appeared in *Forgiveness and Abuse: Jewish and Christian Reflections*, edited by Marie M. Fortune and Joretta Marshall. New York: The Haworth Pastoral Press, 2002.

When Sisters Dream

"You'll never guess what I dreamed last night." Each morning a dream more glorious than the one from the previous night. Each morning one that elevated Josepha above the rest of us. "We were binding sheaves in the fields—"

"When was the last time you bound sheaves? As I recall you're always having your period. As if that's reason enough for our precious little—"

"Judith!" our mother interrupted sharply. She would always come to Josepha's defense.

"Really, Mother, she never does her share of the work."

"I do too. Anyway, we were binding sheaves, and my sheaf rose and stood upright, and your sheaves gathered around it and bowed down to it."

Bedlam broke out among us, one sister hollering that even in her dreams Josepha was insufferable. Another shouting, "If I have to listen to one more of your high and mighty dreams, I'm going to cram a ram's horn down your throat!"

"Why can't you girls get along?" In Mother's voice we heard more a plea than a question.

But the next day was the same.

"You'll never guess what I dreamed last night."

"Another one where we all bow down to Your Majesty?" I asked with sarcasm.

Josepha lifted her chin proudly. "As a matter of fact, the sun, moon, and stars were bowing down to me."

The ten of us hooted. Only Batjamin, the youngest, sat there not understanding what the uproar was about. At least this time Mother scolded Josepha for her arrogance.

Unfazed by Mother's disapproval, she turned to leave the room. "Well, you can't blame a woman for what she dreams, can you?" The rest of us glared after her as she glided away in the colorful robe Mother had woven for her.

"Why don't the rest of us ever have dreams like that?" we asked each other later, as we sheared the sheep. As usual, Josepha had found an excuse not to help.

Ashira said her dreams were filled with embarrassing situations, where her clothes fell off or she forgot how to do an ordinary task, such as drawing water from the well.

Shy Dana confided that hers were dreams of the day. Sometimes she moved among the animals dreaming she conversed with ease, that she was witty and clever in speech.

Judith said nothing, but we all knew, because each night we took turns getting up when she screamed out. Then we would hold her in our arms as she sobbed, wanting her nightmares to cease.

Neither did I speak. There had been a time when I, like Dana, had dreams of the day, where people admired my beauty or my accomplishments. Then as years passed, the demands of physical labor became too much, and I began to dream instead of escape—of a lover, a vast inheritance, any means of getting away I could think of. Until I knew such events would never come to pass, and I gave up dreams of the day altogether.

Those of us who feared our dreams or had abandoned them resented Josepha. It was as if she were empowered by hers, while the rest of us served as receptacles for dreams that either terrified us or left us without hope.

She was walking toward me, her beautiful robe flapping in the wind, her arms outstretched as they so often were, embracing life. Standing at the foot of my mat, she shouted, "Why didn't you stop them?" Her loud voice awakened me.

My intent that day had been simply to scare her, to rid her of her arrogance. It was my sisters who said, "Let's kill her and throw her into one of the pits." As Josepha crouched at our feet, trying to protect her head with her arms, our blows became fiercer. The years of jealousy expressed themselves in a rage we could not control. It was Reba who finally admonished us not to kill Josepha, to instead throw her into a pit. Would we have killed her otherwise? I do not know.

"You're just jealous," Josepha called up to us, "because I'm going to do something with my life, while the bunch of you—you're nothing but a herd of goats. Pathetic goats." I was surprised that after the beating she still had the strength to speak.

"Why don't you take a nap down there—that rock will make a fine pillow—and then tell us about your dream." We all joined in raucous laughter.

Why didn't I stop them? How could I when I couldn't even stop myself?

The beautiful robe walked toward me. No body was beneath its folds, yet it had form. I wanted it. I wanted to wear it and be admired. Closer it came, until I was able to reach out and possess it. But as I tried to put it on, it rose and began to wrap itself around my neck. I sat up with a start, gasping for breath.

I remember the look on her face as I tore the prized garment from her body. My satisfaction when I heard it rip. How I envied her that robe, a birthday gift from Mother, far surpassing any gift I ever received. The years I had tried to please Mother, practically worked my body to its death, and then for Josepha to find favor so easily. Mother's favorite, daughter of her late child-bearing years, the seed planted by her second husband, whom she loved far more than my father.

How easy it was to sell a sister into slavery. To exchange a young woman with extravagant dreams for a handful of silver coins. Dragging her out of the pit into which we had thrown her, we handed her over to a band of Ishmaelites traveling by. Watching the caravan journey on, we joked among ourselves, taking joy in her humiliation.

"Instead of being waited upon by the sun and moon and stars, she'll do the serving."

"She didn't share the burden of work at home. Let her see what work really is like in some distant city where people don't even speak her language. See if anyone there cares about her dreams."

"Oh, no, not my Josepha," Mother wailed when we showed her the robe, torn and splattered with goat's blood. "Not my Josepha." When I saw how sobs racked her body so violently she could scarcely breathe, I took satisfaction in what we had done; for I surmised, perhaps wrongly, that Mother never would have felt such sorrow over my death. Yet a trace of shame crept over me. Shame for making my mother cry, shame for betraying her trust in us.

All ten of us were implicated, so no one dared break the oath of silence. No one dared tell Mother that Josepha was not dead but had been sold as a slave. We let Mother assume the worst.

I was slaughtering a goat, smearing blood on the elegant robe, when suddenly the goat turned into Josepha, and she was wearing her robe, her own blood darkening its colors. Many years had passed since we'd sold her, but the dreams persisted.

We had new worries now, concerns about our family's survival. For several years the winter rains had not come, leaving the fields parched. Without grass we could no longer keep livestock, and with neither grains nor animals we had little to eat. How my heart ached as I watched my sisters' children, who instead of playing their running games, sat quietly, their voices soft. We would not likely live to see another year.

"I have hidden away some coins for a time such as this," Mother said one day. "I hear they have opened the storehouses in Egypt and grain is available. Go down and buy some so we will live and not die."

Carrying empty sacks and the money she had given us, we made the journey, all of us except Batjamin, the youngest of us, who by now had replaced Josepha as Mother's favorite.

The blistering sun made its way nearly all the way across the sky as we stood in line for grain. "Why did we go to all the trouble of making this journey?" we complained among ourselves. "Even if there is enough, the Egyptians surely won't sell to foreigners."

When we finally arrived at the front of the line, we bowed before the governor, our faces to the ground. Looking up, yet not daring to gaze into the woman's face, I saw that her clothing was of the finest fabric, her jewelry expensive. Everything about her—the way she walked, talked, made decisions—it all signified power.

How must I, one who walked among sheep and dressed in coarse material, look to a woman so fine? Surely, I reasoned, she came from an important family and had spent her life among the rich and powerful.

"Who are you?" she demanded to know.

"We are daughters of one woman, twelve of us. The youngest is home with our mother, and another is no longer living."

"You are spies," she accused, her many bracelets jingling as she shook her hand in anger. "You have come to see how weak we have become."

"N-n-no," I stuttered, "we have come to buy grain."

The next three days were filled with confusion, the governor flaunting her power by denying our request yet refusing to let us return home. All the time strutting about, jingling those bracelets. She was obsessed with seeing the family's youngest. How would that convince her we were not spies? Impulsively she had all ten of us jailed, then changed her mind, pledging that if one of us remained as a hostage, the others could return home and bring our youngest sister back to Egypt. The family was starving. We had no choice. We left Simona behind.

Of course Mother resisted our taking Batjamin back to Egypt. She'd lost one daughter and wasn't about to put another's life at risk. And who knew what that crazy governor would do? Yet we knew that unless we returned, and with Batjamin, we would all die. Besides, Simona remained there.

As we presented Batjamin, I boldly gazed for the first time into the woman's face. She looked familiar. I was perplexed by her reaction to seeing Batjamin. The lines on her face softened, her eyes grew misty. How startled I was when she began to weep, shocked yet more when she called through her sobs, "I am Josepha. Is my mother still alive?"

Disbelief—that was my initial reaction. This could not be the sister who had pleaded as we handed her over to the Ishmaelites. If it were, she had not only survived but prospered, accomplishing more than any of us could have—dare I say, *dreamed of?* We pretended to be overjoyed at this reunion, hugging and kissing and shrieking with delight. Pretended because we were, in fact, terrified. The tactics she had used—accusing us of being spies, putting us in jail, keeping Simona hostage until we brought Batjamin—all had been to demonstrate the power she now had over our destiny. I thought back to her dream, the one in which her sheaf stood upright while ours bowed down to it, and recognized this was the event the dream had foretold.

We had renounced our kinship by selling her into slavery. We had sent her to a foreign land, far from her mother whom she loved, far from the traditions of her people. Strangely, she expressed joy in seeing us again, even declared this a time of festivity. Yet while we all clung to each other and shouted words of delight, I was convinced that at any moment the festivities would suddenly stop and she would bring her wrath down upon us.

Instead she said, "Go now, bring Mother, so that our family will survive the famine."

There were, of course, profuse apologies. Though offered with sincerity they were sprinkled with words of justification: "If you hadn't always been bringing up those egotistical dreams. . . At least we didn't kill you." And to our mother: "If you hadn't favored her. . . If you hadn't given her a robe far more beautiful than anything we had . . ."

Our apologies and the tears that accompanied them were for naught. Survival was at stake, Josepha said. Ours and our children's. She made it clear that her generosity was for them, for they had nothing to do with the betrayal. The continuation of our blood line—that was what was important.

I cannot call it reconciliation, the arrangement we worked out. She was clear about that. In an efficient manner she made sure we had the food we needed, that our livestock was fed, that we occupied choice land. Only upon Mother and Batjamin did she shower affection.

When Mother died Josepha mourned beyond the expected time, wailing louder than the rest of us did, obviously feeling a loss, which though shared, we could not fully fathom. The two of them had felt a closeness that did not include us, no matter how much we longed for it. I think Josepha also, more than we, understood Mother's legacy and the significance of her generation passing.

The ten of us feared that with Mother's death Josepha would seek revenge. So we made up another lie: "Before she died Mother told us to tell you that you are to forgive us the evil we did to you." It was the first time the word *forgiveness* had been spoken. I thought it an excellent strategy, for Josepha was certain not to go against Mother's wishes. And we had included *for the evil we did to you,* acknowledging that what we had done was wrong. To make it harder for her to refuse, we fell down on our knees.

Josepha sat before us face buried in her hands, weeping. "Only God can forgive," she finally said. She looked up. Was it my imagination, or did her gaze come to rest on me? "I cannot assuage your guilt. Yes, what you did to me was evil, but God has used that evil for good, so that many people could be kept alive. Don't worry, I will continue to provide for you and your little ones. Only do not ask me to forgive you."

We continued to live together, all of us, but those of us who had betrayed Josepha could not reverse our action. We could not undo selling our sister into slavery.

I still think about the importance of dreams. They are full of mystery, for those that occur in the night come uninvited. Where do they originate? From God? Or do we create our own dreams? Both perhaps.

The mystery surrounding Josepha—murdered, according to the lie we told Mother. All because of her dreams. Yet that which inspired wrath and jealousy among us, her sisters, became her salvation and the source of her power.

Which is perhaps how God turns evil ways to good. By keeping dreams of new possibilities alive.

Better to Have Made the Journey

Exodus 2–16

One day Moses, step-son of the Egyptian princess, goes out and sees the dire conditions under which his people, the Hebrews, are forced to live. After killing an Egyptian who is beating a Hebrew, Moses flees. Much later, as Moses stands beside a burning bush, God tells him that he is to lead the Hebrews to a new land. The journey to the Promised Land is harsh. At times there is no food or water, causing the Hebrews to bicker and complain. Still God leads them, by day in a pillar of cloud, by night in a pillar of fire.

How might Moses, a woman of privilege, have helped her sisters escape their oppressors?

I SELDOM looked up. Meet the eyes of a guard and you were likely to be dragged behind a building and raped, especially if you were young, as I was. So my eyes were to the ground when the disturbance broke out: a woman's curse shattering the monotonous grunts of those of us lifting and pulling and pushing. The angry shouts of men. Furtively glancing out the corner of my eye, I caught a glimpse of a gold-trimmed robe disappearing around a corner.

"Keep moving," we were ordered.

Usually the corpses we stepped over belonged to our sisters who had fallen from exhaustion or malnourishment. This time we were shocked to see the dead body of a guard.

In the days that followed whispers passed among us. Mosiah, step-daughter of the princess, had heaved a rock at a guard and killed him. She had fled the city, a regiment of soldiers in pursuit. The king was furious, came the word from those who worked in the palace. "After all I've done for her," he'd been heard to say. "I should have known she'd turn out to be like the rest of them." *The rest of them* referring to women like me, foreign women who had for generations lived in captivity.

One of us by birth, Mosiah had been spared our oppression through the cleverness of her mother, who had left the infant where the king's daughter was known to bathe. Finding the baby by the stream, believing it had been abandoned, the princess's heart warmed to it, so that she felt compelled to take the girl back to the palace. Soon Mosiah's mother appeared, offering her services as a wet-nurse. Thus it happened that, with her mother watching over her, the child grew up in the royal household yet learned about the circumstances of her birth and who her kinswomen were.

Those of us not fortunate enough to be transformed into royalty had been sentenced to a life of hardship. From dawn to dusk we made bricks and hauled them on our backs. All the while men stood over us, shouting curses, threatening us with closed fists, oft times reaching out to strike us with a whip.

So what led to Mosiah's killing a man? we asked among ourselves. Why would she take such a risk?

Later she told us she had been restless, a voice within urging her to venture from the palace. Go *out,* the voice said, and look upon the travail of your kinswomen. Mosiah preferred to stay *in* where she felt secure and comfortable. The voice persisted, however, until she felt no choice but to quietly steal from the royal household.

What she saw astounded her: women, young and old, bent under heavy burdens, our hands swollen by wounds that cracked and bled. She could not help but cry over the embedded scars of sorrow on our faces. We were her sisters. Suddenly a guard yelled at one of us and thrashed his whip upon her back. Cursing, Mosiah picked up a rock and hurled it at him.

While her behavior startled even her, it infuriated us, for it only made our situation worse. The following day we were forced to make and carry twice as many bricks as we had in the days before. We now hated her: a woman of privilege whose sympathies were not welcome.

She was able to flee; we had no choice but to stay.

No one recognized her. Years had passed, years she'd spent in a distant country. Those who had sought Mosiah's death had themselves died and the land was ruled by different men. Although her hair had grayed and she now wore a simple garment instead of fine clothes, her bearing gave evidence of having grown up in the royal household. Unlike the rest of us whose shoulders were stooped, she stood straight and walked with dignity. There was about her a gentle strength, seen most clearly in the eyes and the soft lines of her face.

"The God of your mothers has sent me to free you," she told us. We laughed among ourselves, for though she spoke our tongue, she had the oppressor's accent. She was one of us, she said, her tone conciliatory.

"*Who* sent you?" we asked suspiciously.

"The God of your grandmothers and their mothers before them. She says to tell you that she has seen your oppression and will take you from this land to one flowing with milk and honey."

"So," I said to her, "this God of our ancestors, who ignored our mothers' and our grandmothers' cries of pain, she is suddenly interested in our plight?" Around me I heard the mumbled assents of the others. "Get out of here," I ordered. "We want nothing to do with you. If the guards come, we are the ones who will be beaten, not you."

A woman who spoke like our oppressor, whose comportment was refined and gentle—she was claiming to be one of us? She was going to free us? How presumptuous, to believe after only a glimpse of the brutal treatment we received that she understood the torture of our lives.

For days and days Mosiah tried to reason with us. Despite our disdain, she did not give up. After we kept refusing to listen to her, she brought along her sister, Aaronit, who did most of the talking. God, Aaronit said, had looked down upon our afflictions. "Everything's going to get better," she assured us in accent like our own.

Everything's going to get better? Not words to be believed by women long held in captivity. Try to escape and we were likely to get caught, beaten even more harshly than before. Yet as Aaronit continued speaking, her words became persuasive, and in spite of our misgivings we found ourselves warming to her zeal.

And gradually we began to trust Mosiah. Not because of anything she said, for Aaronit did most of the talking, but because she did not leave. We reminded each other that years earlier she could have chosen to stay in the royal household. Instead she had stepped out to witness our suffering. As we whispered about her courage and determination, we began to feel the flutter of something we'd never felt before: hope.

Sprigs of hope do not suddenly grow into trees of confidence. God had a plan, Mosiah and Aaronit told us. Mosiah would implore the king and his magistrate to allow us to go into the wilderness to engage in religious rituals. We knew our tormentors would never permit us to be out of their sight. Yet if anyone was able to persuade them, it would be Mosiah, who spoke their language and knew how to follow the decorum of the court, qualities abhorrent to us but surely impressive to our oppressors.

Mosiah's first meeting with the king and magistrates, however, did not go well. "Please, sirs," she said in a most beguiling feminine voice, "we respectfully request that the women be allowed to practice the rituals whereby they honor their God."

Instead of treating her respectfully, the men immediately formed a circle around her. Moving nearer and nearer, they made lewd remarks and laughed. When they were quite close, they shouted into her face, "Why do they need to perform the rituals now when they haven't in the past?" The answer, of course, was that they and their ancestors had done all within their power to separate us from our God, punishing our foremothers' efforts to keep the traditions alive, until all that remained were vague ideas of how the rituals were to be performed.

The king and magistrates accused Mosiah of trying to trick them. "If the women have enough time to go out of the city for their rituals, they must not be working hard enough." Not only did they deny the request, they increased our workload, and instead of furnishing straw for the bricks as they had done in the past, they forced us to search for it ourselves, while still expecting us to produce bricks at the same rate. The guards beat and swore at us even more than they had before.

I cursed the day Mosiah had entered our lives. The glimmer of hope I'd briefly held was an illusion, I was convinced. If this God of my foremothers did indeed exist, if she wanted me to be free, why wait until now?

"It would have been better had you never returned," we shouted at Mosiah and Aaronit.

A change came over Mosiah. The fiery spirit that had briefly flared when she'd heaved the rock at the guard began to exhibit itself again. The soft lines of her face gave way to a firm jaw, intense hard eyes. She gained confidence in speaking. It was in this frame of mind that she returned to the king and magistrates, taking Aaronit with her. This time there was no "we respectfully request"; the two *demanded* that we be allowed to practice our rituals out of the city.

"When will the foreign women understand that I am their God?" the king asked. "I am the one who decides their fate."

"If you do not allow them to practice their rituals, the God of their grandmothers and great-grandmothers will change the water of the river into blood," Mosiah and Aaronit threatened.

"I am sooo frightened," the king mocked. The magistrates howled with laughter.

Then, in the presence of the king and his magistrates, Aaronit lifted her staff. Not until later did the men discover that at that moment the river began to flow with menstrual blood. Soon all the fish had died and a terrible stench spread throughout the city. Still the men who ruled over us would not give in.

It was a simple request, was it not, that we be allowed to go out of the city to practice our rituals? Instead of yielding, however, the king and his magistrates held firm, clearly enjoying the opportunity to exercise their power. In fact, though, they were enabling God to better demonstrate her might.

While those of us who had lived our lives under oppression could not conceive of escaping, Mosiah, because she had grown up free, did not see the impossibility of her mission. It became her will against the king's. Rather God's will against the king's.

Unwilling to accept defeat, Mosiah and Aaronit constantly rushed from one place to another: to the king and magistrates, who would adamantly refuse our petition; then to us with words of encouragement, which we sometimes believed but often did not; then back to God saying, "The women are discouraged and the men won't bend, so what are we going to do?"

Upon God's instructions, Mosiah and Aaronit would return to us, again vowing that we were going to escape bondage, then race back to tell the king and magistrates that since the menstrual blood hadn't changed their hearts, maybe a plague of frogs or mosquitoes or boils would.

While they tired of traveling back and forth, we women grew weary of promises. God had been promising to take us to a safe place. What was her word worth if she'd allowed generations before us to live in captivity? Mosiah had been promising to stay with us, not give up the cause. She'd get tired, we assumed, and return to her comfortable exile. The king even promised that if we gave up on our demand, the overseers would change their behavior, become kind. We recognized the worthlessness of that promise.

As women in captivity, we had no power to make promises. Having never had control over our lives, we were unable to see a future in which we might choose our commitments.

Our morale fluctuated. One day we'd speak of solidarity; the next day we'd mumble among ourselves that there was no way we were going to ever taste freedom. At times we refused to listen to Mosiah and Aaronit. Their interference was only leading to more severe punishment.

By now the king and magistrates, who had gathered even more like-minded men around them, openly declared that a group of women would never get the best of them. Weren't they, after all, men of power? Because of their refusal, though, God destroyed herds throughout the land and decimated crops. Yet all the while the king and his men proclaimed they were well on the way to victory.

How many plagues does it take to convince a man that it's time to give in? In this situation ten, each plague more severe than the previous. Forced to take even more drastic measures, God finally resorted to the worst: She struck dead the first born of every household, even the king's oldest child.

Only then did the king and his men realize this was a contest they could not win. Suddenly they were urging us to leave the city. Immediately. "Include us in your supplications," they begged, "so that when you return we can all live in harmony."

But it had never been God's intent that we perform our rituals then return to our captors. No, she had promised us freedom. Accompanied by our children, we permanently left the land of our subjugation and headed for that safe place she'd promised us.

Wide-eyed I looked to my left and to my right. Walls of water on both sides. How could we know they wouldn't come crashing down? But to turn around was to come face-to-face with the oppressors who now knew they had been outsmarted. To turn around was to give ourselves over to them. We'd come too far.

Past the walls of water, we marched into the wilderness. Because God knew that years of subjugation had left our bodies and spirits broken, she did not have Mosiah lead us straight to the place she had in mind. That would have required us to confront new enemies. No, instead of a direct route, we followed one of zigs and zags, sharp curves, even blockades. Each new challenge was a crisis, occasionally making conditions better, more often making them worse.

To go where you've never been means there are no familiar landmarks, no places where you know you can hide if the necessity arises. Darkness is the worst part, since walking toward freedom allows little nighttime rest. Even if a pillar of fire leads, you usually can't see where you step or what unseen creatures lurk. So we journeyed in fear.

We worried too that we would die from lack of food and water. Once we went three days with no water, and when we finally found a spring, the water was bitter. Our tears of disappointment were bitter too, so we named the place Bitterness.

We marched on, Mosiah leading. An unsettling responsibility she said, for she didn't know where we were or how we'd recognize our destination when we got there. And she had to endure our complaints. "At least we had security before," we whined, "a place to sleep, food to eat." When the children cried, we tried to comfort them, telling them we would soon be in that safe place, trying to convince ourselves as much as them.

On empty stomachs we marched. Once when our pace became little more than a crawl and I was about to lay my body on the ground to designate the place of my burial, a melody sprang up. In a child's voice. Another voice picked up the tune, then another and another, until the entire brigade of women and children were singing,

You will bring us to your own mountain.

The place, O God, which will be our new home.

That evening God brought us quails to eat, and the next morning bread lay like dew upon the ground. From then on we often journeyed with the song on our lips, confident now that God would provide for us. So that as our sojourn extended, as year after year passed, we were able to maintain faith that someday we would arrive at our destination.

Mosiah did not live to reach the safe place God had promised. Before she died, however, God led her to the mountain top and invited her to look out over the land where we and our descendents would dwell. Until the end, her vision remained keen, her vigor undiminished, the fire in her eyes as bright as the fire's coals. She had stood up to kings; men had defied her at their own peril. For thirty days we celebrated her life among us.

What did I learn from the pilgrimage? What do any of us learn in a lifetime?

As one chosen to lead after Aaronit's death, I learned that I have gifts I never would have believed I had. In spite of earlier misgivings, I've discovered in my old age that my words have power and that I have the ability to serve as a mediator on God's behalf.

Once you've taken on an adversary, you learn to stay on guard. I've learned that too, to be wary. That even though we're now in a safe place, safety is always tentative.

I learned how to survive—we all learned that. We survive not through manners and sweetness but sometimes by calling plagues down upon those who oppress us. Even among ourselves, we've become intolerant of sugary pleasantries, for to be overly pleasant is to deny that the hardships we faced ever happened.

Milk and honey, God promised. While I wouldn't accuse her of breaking the promise, I'd say she exaggerated. But then maybe I read more into it than she intended. I assumed she meant luxury; apparently she didn't, since our survival depends on working hard. But our labors are for ourselves and those we love.

Evenings we sit by the fire and tell the stories of how we came to this place, of the near tragedies and the glorious surprises, of what we left and what we found. We've become a group of crusty women whose laughter is raucous, whose tears bring back memories of Bitterness. Our greatest joys are to be with each other and to know that each woman's survival is a bane to those who would have kept her in oppression.

Never do any of us speak of wanting to go back. We've learned that it is far better to have made the journey—thirst, hunger, terror and all—than to have spent the rest of our lives in captivity.

The Wall

Joshua 6

An unusual siege it is. For six days the Israelites circle the walls of Jericho. On the seventh they let out a mighty shout, and the walls tumble down.

Out of distrust of strangers and foreigners, women continue to build walls.

THE WALL had been built long before any of us was born. Strong it was, baked by the hot sun. So high and thick that surely no enemy could penetrate it.

It was there to make us feel secure, our mothers and grandmothers told us. To protect us from foreign women who begged outside the gate and lived beyond the fields of wild grain. They spoke another language, worshipped another god. They neither observed our rules of cleanliness nor dressed as we did.

In spite of the wall, we felt vulnerable. We were convinced that the foreign women yearned for our objects of silver and gold, our garments of silk and fine linen. The spring we drew from each day—surely they coveted its abundant flow. Fearing that the strangers might kill us to gain possession of our goods and our spring, we placed sentries atop the wall. All through the day and night they kept watch lest the undesirable women, protected by darkness, try to enter our town.

Even with sentries we did not feel safe. So we extended the wall's height, placed on top of it sharp objects, which were baked into the clay. Each of us armed ourselves.

Still we did not feel secure.

Almost daily we ventured outside the wall to collect grains for daily use and for storing in case we had to endure a lengthy siege. As we passed the strangers begging outside our gate, we averted our eyes, pretending not to notice them. Sometimes we motioned with our hand that they were to step aside as we passed. We would then go about our tasks as if the women did not exist—though our fears reminded us they did.

One day when I climbed to the top of the wall to look out over the land, I observed a cloud of sand in the distant wilderness. Closer it came until I saw that it was not merely a cloud of sand but the foreign women marching side by side, row upon row of them moving toward our town. I ran to tell neighbors and friends, who returned with me, weapons ready to defend our homes.

Peering over the top of the wall, we were perplexed by what we saw. Instead of storming our defenses, the foreign women merely marched. In ordered columns they circled our town, eerily silent except for the pounding of their feet upon the ground and the trumpeting of rams' horns. After only one time around the wall, they marched off toward the river.

Frantically we sent our scouts to learn of the strangers' intent. Upon returning, the scouts reported that the women had built an altar to their god and that they practiced strange rituals.

The next day, at the same time, the foreign women again approached in ordered columns. Again, they circled the town one time. From our hiding places atop the wall, we strained our ears to hear them speak, but as before, only the pounding of their feet and the blare of the rams' horns broke the silence.

On the third day they repeated their march.

We grew more fearful. What was their plan? One lone voice among us suggested that we might assume good intentions and invite the women inside. We could welcome them to our tables and share our provisions. Someone else suggested that we bring them inside to become our servants. No, many insisted, we should keep them out altogether, for their walking around our wall surely signaled evil intentions.

A fourth day the foreigners formed their columns and circled our wall. A fifth day. A sixth day.

The wall's limitations now became evident, for though it kept the foreigners out, it also trapped us inside. After the second day of peering from the top of the wall at the foreign women marching, we had ceased going beyond it to gather grain, fearful of an ambush. Inside the tension mounted, causing us to argue with each other over what we should do.

The waiting, the unbearable waiting.

On the seventh day, before daybreak, I was awakened from a restless sleep by sentries reporting that again the women were outside the wall. This time, rather than circling our town once then leaving, they marched around it and around it and around it. Only the simultaneous landing of their feet upon the earth and the trumpeting of rams' horns broke the morning stillness. Perhaps the wall was not too high to climb over, we worried among ourselves; perhaps it was not impenetrable. We gathered our collection of weapons and nervously waited for the women to storm the wall.

Suddenly all of them shouted with such force that the ground shook: "In the name of God!"

The most amazing thing happened. The wall trembled. Slowly the bottom of one section began to crumble, the stones atop it cascading to the ground. Then the adjoining section, followed by the next, then the next, until the entire wall had tumbled to the ground.

The collapse of our defenses so terrified us that instead of fighting, we could only fall to our knees and beg for mercy.

I often wonder whether we would have been as compassionate had we been the ones kept outside all those years. We expected the foreign women to raid our town, steal our possessions of value, perhaps slaughter us. Instead they immediately set to work clearing the rubble.

HAD EVE COME FIRST AND JONAH BEEN A WOMAN

"Take the other end," one of them said to me, motioning with her hand that I should pick up the opposite side of a large chunk. Hesitatingly I stepped toward her, looking into her eyes for some sign of animosity. I saw none. I lifted the end of the dusty fragment, and together we carried it away from the town to a pit where all the wall's pieces were being tossed.

After many days all of the rubble had been cleared away. Now all women freely walked back and forth between the grain fields and drew water from the spring that had been ours alone. Sometimes I walked with my kin; at other times I walked alongside those who had courageously knocked down our wall.

And You Will Eat of the Honey

Judges 13–16

As one consecrated to God, Samson is superior in many ways. He has a keen intellect and enjoys posing riddles. His physical strength is both envied and feared. Determined to learn the source of his power, the Philistines, who rule over Judah, tell Delilah, the woman Samson loves, to seduce him and learn the secret of his strength. Discovering that his strength depends on his hair remaining uncut, the Philistines cut it off and gouge out his eyes. When his hair begins to grow back, he is able to bring down the house where all the Philistine lords are gathered. He too dies.

Many women have experienced attempts to rob them of their power.

WHEN DID I first recognize they were trying to take my power away, you ask. You know, don't you, that we're never fully aware of our power until it's challenged.

I must have been eleven or twelve years old. Until then I took delight in my exceptional skills, winning every contest, whether it was one requiring athletic prowess or intelligence. It was a period of gathering my power through discoveries that come with incessant questions and curiosity. Nothing could harness my intellect or diminish my zeal. My energy had no limit, or so Mother thought until I dropped exhausted on my mat at night.

But you ask when I first recognized they were trying to take my power *away*. I remember the afternoon clearly. Several elders waited for me as I returned from the fields where I'd been searching for the plant Mother needed for a poultice. They waited along the path they knew I must take to get home, behind the rocks so that I did not see them until they sprang upon me.

It was not a good idea to be learning the things I was learning, they told me as they formed a circle around me. Better to be practicing the arts that would make me a good wife and mother so that our people's ways might last for generations. Though startled by the fierceness in their eyes and the harshness of their tones, I was not frightened. With words provided by God, I spoke as one many times my years, overpowering the elders' arguments. Then calmly I broke through their circle and returned home.

But their reproach left me perplexed. I knew that in games I was always chosen to lead, and it was clear to me that I was quicker of mind than any of my peers. I had assumed all of that was good. Why then would anyone see it as a problem?

Back home I told Mother of the encounter. "The old lions," she said angrily, "fearful someone will challenge them. But they are no contest for you. Someday bees will gather in their carcasses, and you will eat of the honey."

That was the first time I had a sense of my strength. Because someone tried to take it away.

My mother? You want to know what she was like? Her name will be forgotten, even by those who establish reputations for remembering minute details. *A barren woman* will be the words used to identify her, marking her as one who resisted her gender's role.

Everyone who knew her marveled that such an ordinary woman should have given birth to such a remarkable child, for people of our town recognized neither her gifts nor her quiet strength. But ordinary she was not. Stooping over in the fields, lifting large bundles of grain, managing our compound so that the dietary laws were obeyed—she carried out her varied responsibilities. But as she labored, she collected the wisdom of the earth, paying special attention to the healing powers of plants.

No, she was not ordinary. Though powerless among our people, she was strong of will, attuned to the secrets of nature. Because of her devotion to creation, an angel of God spoke to her. Directly. Said she'd been chosen to conceive and bear me, a daughter. On the day of my birth my mother consecrated me to God.

Extraordinary woman giving birth to an extraordinary daughter is how her life should be remembered. I have not forgotten her or anything she began teaching me as soon as I was able to understand: what herbs to collect, how to touch an injury, how to draw a newborn from the womb. Every day I worked alongside her, gathering from her the wisdom of generations. She taught me to develop the sharp eye, the sensitive nose, the alert ear. She passed on to me her wisdom.

My mother passed on her strength.

The elders, did they bother me again, you want to know. Oh yes. Though after a while they quit being so direct and instead subtly spread resentment against me. Manipulated my friends.

For example, I found great pleasure in making up riddles. Whenever our people gathered around the fire, I created mental puzzles and watched brows wrinkle in thought.

"If I'm your best friend," Adah said to me one afternoon as we ground meal, "tell me the answer to today's riddle." To assure her that she was indeed my best friend, I told her, only to find out later that the elders had put her up to asking me. With stealth she returned to them and whispered the answer. That night my people met around the fire, telling stories and challenging each other with mental puzzles. When I repeated the riddle I had posed the night before, everyone shouted the answer.

Their laughter left me feeling belittled and wounded. I wasn't the only person who told riddles. Why was I the one everyone most wanted to defeat? Did they think I flaunted my intelligence? Perhaps I was not special after all but a foolish girl whose pride kept urging her to outsmart others.

HAD EVE COME FIRST AND JONAH BEEN A WOMAN

As I awaited sleep, as my eyes stared out into the darkness, the spirit of God came upon me. I recognized it as it filled my heart and mind, giving me strength and wisdom that went beyond the normal.

But from that night forward I no longer posed riddles.

You want to know how a woman comes to have so many enemies. By exercising her power, I would say; yes when a woman begins to use her power, she begins to garner enemies.

As I matured, my wisdom increased, and my power became known even beyond our town. When my mother and father died, I stayed on in the family compound, which became a busy place, with women coming to me for healing and guidance. They brought their children for special blessings too.

All the while, though, the elders talked among themselves against me. Whether out of envy or fear, I do not know. Of this I am sure: They had no reason to fear me. I only wanted to use the gifts God had provided, the knowledge my mother had bequeathed.

But the men tried to stop me. First they ordered their wives to stay away, and when that failed, they burned down my compound. They thought they would destroy my power by destroying the place where I mixed my herbs and prayed my prayers of healing.

There's an advantage to knowing who your enemies are, I discovered: You are forced to develop cunning, which is quite different from intelligence. The cunning woman is watchful, alert to danger. To become cunning, I first had to learn not to trust; for everyone, even those who called me friend, was set upon bringing me down. I had to take great care not to show the slightest vulnerability, for like a lame sheep a vulnerable woman becomes easy prey for the lion.

Within me cunning and wrath now dwelled.

I learned to weaken my enemies before they could harm me. Keep them too busy to plot my destruction, I decided. I began to bring pestilence upon their fields so their energies would go into replanting.

"What are you doing?" women demanded. "Don't you know they are rulers over us? The harm you do by damaging their crops, you do to us too." I did not tell them that out of my new-found cunning, I now recognized they had become my enemies as well.

As watchful as I was, I was taken by surprise one day when I found myself surrounded by a horde of clamoring men carrying spears and axes and calling for my death. Give me something with which I might defend myself, I prayed to God. I looked down. At my feet lay the dried jawbone of an ass. Whirling it around my head, I started to whisper incantations. Slowly the men stepped back and walked away from me toward their own dwellings. As the last one turned from me, I flung my weapon aside. I call the place The Hill of the Jawbone.

The incident at The Hill of the Jawbone was no victory, however. Against their husbands' wishes women continued to seek my counsel and healing, but as soon as they left my presence, they spoke against me. Those I considered my closest friends regularly questioned the source of my power. When they reported back to the elders that it came from God, the elders said that could not be so; its origins, they claimed, were in darkness.

Loneliness. You ask me to speak of the loneliness that accompanies power. Yes, loneliness created its own kind of vulnerability, something I had not anticipated. So that when a man came into our town, a stranger, and offered friendship, I trusted him too quickly. Unlike everyone else, who was bent on destroying my power, he affirmed it. The hours we spent together were filled with laughter, and for the first time I knew the joy of loving a man. I told him everything about myself—my history, my dreams.

He stood beside me as I healed the sick. He held out the ointment, offered the cup. Day after day he never left my side, speaking softly to me when one woman or child moved away and another approached. As I watched him quiet the children with his gentle voice, I vowed to myself that I would someday nurture his child in my womb.

One day he mentioned the power I gained from *him*; the next day he referred to *our* partnership. The day after that I let it pass when he said that without him I would be unable to do my work. At first I silently disagreed, but as time went on, I began to think, yes, he is right, without him I would be powerless.

Then his question. A simple one, it seemed the first time he asked it, as we lay spent from our lovemaking. "Where does your power come from?"

"From you," I playfully answered.

"Seriously," he said the following night, "where does your power come from?"

"From you," I again answered. "Seriously."

A third night he asked, "Where does your power come from?"

This time I was moved by his strong desire to know. "From you!" I threw myself at his feet, convinced that what I said was true.

The next morning I found that he had left me, disappeared into the night like a stolen jewel. I felt as if my life had been taken from me. For days I stayed inside, eyes closed. All was dark as I gazed into the abyss of my own mind. I plunged its depths in search of my power, but it had vanished, escaped with the one I had come to believe was its source. I wanted to end my life but lacked the strength to do even that alone.

I often wonder how I survived the long, long period of desolation.

How did I recover my power, you want to know. Well, one day a woman's voice called into my compound. "We need you," she said. "Come with your healing power. A plague has fallen upon our households, and our children die."

I did not reply, choosing to remain in the dark world of my mind. But the following day, other women joined the first and called to me, "Please, please come. Use your power to save our people."

It was not my vanity that drew me from the mat, but the hand of God pulling me out into the light. Outside my compound scores of women and children awaited me, each of them begging for my help. But I have no power, I wanted to say.

Instead of speaking, however, I returned to my dwelling, where I sat for a while on the hard earth of the courtyard. Legs crossed, eyes searching the heavens, I began to feel it returning. The power. Flowing through my fingers, up my arms and legs, expanding beneath my breasts, traveling up my neck. Why should I use it to help those who had been so eager to turn against me? Briefly I was tempted to use it vengefully, much as I had during the days I destroyed crops.

No, the spirit of God was upon me. I rose and stepped from my compound, prepared to bring healing to those who needed it.

The Road to Ramah

I Samuel 1–15

Hannah promises that if God will lend her a child, she will lend the child back to God. When her son, Samuel, is weaned, she delivers him to the temple, where he grows up under the care and tutelage of Eli, an elderly priest. As a child, Samuel is the one chosen by God to tell Eli that he and his children will be punished for his sons' iniquity. Later, as a trusted leader who administers justice, Samuel learns that like the sons of Eli, his own are unfit to serve God.

Many of today's mothers of faith grieve over their children turning away from God.

As SELA carried out her daily tasks at the temple, she paid close attention to every ritual and listened carefully to each incantation. Those who visited the temple admired her industriousness, but they considered her peculiar. *Abandoned by her mother at an early age,* some said. *It is as if she's in her own world. Strange child, strange child.*

Only with Elisheba, the priestess to whom Sela had been delivered when barely weaned, could the girl converse with ease. Though practically blind, Elisheba could see into Sela's heart and understand her longings.

Evenings, right before she dropped off in sleep, Sela would beg Elisheba to retell the story of how she had come to live at the temple. "One day I was sitting beside the door when your mother came in. I thought she had—"

"Why, why did you think she had drunk too much wine?" the child would interrupt.

"She moved her lips, yet no sounds came from her mouth," Elisheba said. "When I told her to put away her wine, she assured me she had not been drinking but that she was quite distressed."

"Why was she distressed?"

"I did not know at the time. Later I learned it was because she had no children. More than anything, she wanted a daughter. At the time, though, I saw only that she was distraught and my heart could not help but join in her sorrow. As she was about to leave the temple, I placed my hand on her shoulder and said, 'May God grant your petition.'

"I quickly forgot about her. Then, a few years later, here comes your mother, and what do you think she has in her arms?"

"Me," Sela would say, almost in a whisper.

"Right. She reminded me that I had blessed her. She had prayed for a daughter and God gave her one."

"What did she say when she brought me here?" Sela wanted to hear the reassuring words again.

"She said, 'More than anything in this world, I love my daughter. I know that God has plans for her. Her father and I do not have the ability to prepare her for such greatness, but you do. As great a sorrow as it gives me, for her sake, I must bring her here so that you can nurture her to become the woman God wants her to be. The only way I can bear to part with her is if I think of it as a loan. As long as she lives, she will be loaned to God.'"

Then Sela would ask what it meant to be loaned to God. Elisheba could never answer the question to the girl's satisfaction.

Later, after Elisheba had left Sela's side, Sela would wonder: How could a mother give her own daughter away? No, Hannah did not *give* her daughter to God, Elisheba had assured her, Hannah *loaned* her.

Who did she belong to then? Not to God; God was borrowing her. Not to her mother, at least not anymore; her mother had brought her to the temple. Not to Elisheba; Elisheba had sons and daughters of her own, all of them adults. Sela would fall asleep wishing to belong to somebody.

Once a year, when Hannah made the journey to Shiloh to offer the annual sacrifice, Sela had the opportunity to see her mother. Each time Hannah presented her daughter with a new robe. During their brief time together, the girl did not know what to say to this woman who loved her yet had given her away. When it was time for taking leave, Elisheba would extend a special blessing upon Hannah, because she had loaned her first daughter to God, Elisheba said. Later, believing that her mother's spirit dwelled in every stitch, Sela would run her fingers across the new robe. Over and over again. Being loaned to God was supposed to be a blessing, but it didn't feel like one.

Sela grew up loving this woman who clung to her when it was time to return home, a woman connected to her by blood.

Who knows why some hear the voices and others do not? Perhaps God speaks to only a few. Perhaps God speaks often, but only those who are attentive hear when their name is called. Could it be that God speaks most often to children, who trust their senses and have little notion of distinguishing between what is *real* and what is imagined? Or could it be that God chooses to speak directly to those who feel the most alone, those who cry themselves to sleep at night because they believe they belong to no one?

Late one night, when the girl was sleeping inside the temple, the sound of her own name awakened her. "Sela, Sela," she heard. She assumed it was the voice of Elisheba. Sela did not consider staying curled up in her blanket, but rose and raced to Elisheba. "Here I am. Here I am, for you called."

Awakened from a deep sleep, Elisheba rolled over. "I did not call," she said. "Go lie down."

Back on her mat, gazing over at the Lamp of God, which had not yet gone out, Sela wondered what she had heard. Then she saw the lamp flame flicker as if a breeze passed over it. She peered beyond it to see if someone had entered the room. The only sound she heard was the scratching of an animal.

Just as she was about to drift back to sleep, the voice came to her once more. "Sela, Sela."

Again she rushed to Elisheba's side. "Here I am, for you called me."

"I did not call. Go lie down," Elisheba said gently.

Returning to her mat, Sela lay on her back looking up into the darkness. This was a night of importance; she could feel it in her body. She was ready to jump up again, should the voice return.

And return it did. "Sela, Sela." Up from the mat she leaped. "Here I am," she told Elisheba, "for I'm sure you called me."

It was then, after the third call, that Elisheba understood. "Go lie down," she instructed the girl, "and if your name is called again, answer, 'Speak, God, for I am listening.'" This Sela did.

So began a lifetime of dialogue between the two of them, Sela and God.

But that night, in their first conversation, God's words were difficult for a girl to understand. They were merciless words against her old, nearly blind step-mother. Elisheba's daughters, God said, had closed their minds and hearts to the needs of the people and were selfishly demanding the best offerings for themselves. In spite of God's promise to Elisheba's mother, the family line of priestesses would end, and because Elisheba had not restrained her daughters, they would soon die. God had threatened before; now the threat would be carried out.

Yesterday Sela had been a child, under the authority of Elisheba. *Was this part of becoming a woman?* she wondered as she lay in the darkness. To be given information you would rather not have, to be forced to speak a truth that would bring sorrow to one you loved, to have responsibilities you never asked for thrust upon you? She did not want to be placed in a position of power over the one who had nurtured and taught her.

When morning came she tried to avoid Elisheba. Finally, though, she heard, "Come, child, come tell me what God said to you." According to God's instructions, the girl reluctantly told of the punishment in store for Elisheba and her daughters. As long as she lived, she would remember Elisheba's cries of distress and her own intense sorrow over being the one to deliver the message.

From that night on God favored Sela, this loaned one. And because she waited for God's words and listened intently when they came, her wisdom increased.

Because God's children communicate in earthly tongues, a mediator is often needed, one who can explain the ways of God to the people and speak to God on their behalf.

Sela was such a mediator. She traveled the land, admonishing the people to be faithful, offering advice for living justly and honoring creation. When the people made sacrifices and offered prayers of thanksgiving, she intoned words she knew God would understand.

One afternoon she was about to leave a town in which she had told a man where to find his lost goat and settled several disputes, one related to a woman who had promised her son in marriage to two families. By the town gate she overheard some women talking. "How is it," one of them said, "that God speaks to Sela of what we should do, but gives her no guidance on how to direct her own sons and daughters?"

Pretending she had heard nothing, Sela rushed home toward Ramah. Her shoulders tense, her fists clenched, she spoke to herself in rapid sentences as she walked. "No guidance on how to direct her own sons and daughters? Why of course I instructed them—from the time they could speak."

"Sela, ah, Sela," she heard.

She caught her breath then exhaled slowly. "Speak God, for your servant hears."

"It is time to face the truth. Your children blaspheme my name and worship other gods."

"But they are yet young," she reminded God. "With maturity they will see their waywardness and turn to you."

"Sela," God said, "they have children of their own. When will maturity arrive? When they are eighty?"

"They are growing in spiritual stature. Really. The youngest, she gives alms to the poor."

"Only when someone is watching; then she returns and forces the person to return the coins. Your children have no sympathy for widows and the poor and give bribes to those in power."

Sela took a seat on a nearby rock and stared into the distance. Tears filled her eyes. "I have tried so hard," she said. "What did I do wrong?"

"It is a question I have been asking myself for centuries. We take a risk, you know, when we bring them into the world." God heaved a heavy sigh.

Still seated on the rock, Sela pushed sand into a small mound with the toe of her sandal. "But who will take my place when I am gone? My eldest, she is the one who should."

"She is attuned to neither me nor the people, only to her own selfish whims."

All was quiet between them until finally God spoke. "A baby is born. A girl, a boy. More than anything I want my children to love me. They do at first, but as they get older they decide my commandments are capricious. They are convinced I want to control their behavior, when in fact my intent has always been to help them live in harmony with each other."

"Have my children rebelled against you or against me?"

"Both of us, I think."

"Is there anything we can do?"

"That too is a question I keep asking myself. I have no answer. We take a risk when we bring them into the world, and again when we give them freedom. Unfortunately we cannot protect them from the consequences of their decisions."

They remained quiet for some time. Sela stared into the distance without seeing.

God broke the silence. "As a child you struggled with the question of who you belonged to. You have long thought that I chose you, which I did. But you chose to belong to me as well. You listened for my voice, and your heart leaned toward me. So too your children have made a choice. They have decided to belong to nothing but their own greed."

Sela rose from the rock. Evening approached and the arid land was cooling, sending shivers across her body. She resumed her journey homeward, God walking beside her. They continued their conversation, speaking of motherhood's sorrows. Sela spoke of her regret that her children did not love the God of their mother, the God of their history. God told how she mourned her children choosing selfishness and hard-heartedness over generosity and compassion.

By the time they reached the town gates, Sela understood what God the mother had known for generations: that if her children were going to love freely, they would have to decide for themselves to whom they belonged.

Let None of Us Be Cowards

1 Samuel 17

The Philistines and the Israelites are prepared for battle. From the camp of the Philistines steps Goliath, a giant of a man, who challenges the Israelites to send out a man to fight him. David, a young shepherd, responds, and with only a slingshot slays Goliath.

Some women bravely take on the giants of the world.

"Hey girls, come fight with me. If you win, I'll be your servant. If I win"—his deep laugh echoes across the valley—"you'll be my servants."

"Who's that?" I ask my sisters as I hand over the bread Mother told me to bring them.

"If you didn't spend all your time lolling out in the fields and playing your lyre, you'd know that's the most powerful man in the land."

"Is he nicer than he sounds?"

"Nice! Whatever gives you that idea?"

"All those women standing around him." I'm thinking I might want to be near him too, if the opportunity presents itself.

"Foolish girl, that's because they lost."

"They must like him though, or they wouldn't stay."

"Foolish girl," they repeat in unison, each one shaking her head in disgust.

"Come on, girls," he calls again, his feet planted far apart, his arm lifted high. "Come on, I promise; if you win, I'll be your servant."

While his bellowing laugh causes my sisters to pull back in fear, I decide to steal across the valley for a closer look. Moving in and out of shadows, sometimes crawling on my hands and knees, I make my way toward him. Now I've seen powerful men before, I decide from my vantage point behind a bush, but nobody like this. His frame dominates the landscape, and he wears the trappings of power: a heavy coat of mail and greaves of bronze upon his legs. I observe how arrogantly he governs the women who surround him, telling them to go fetch this and go fetch that. One polishes his shield, another serves him a drink.

On the women's faces I see defeat, and my heart cries out. No man should have this kind of power.

Making my way back to my sisters, again in a manner most cautious, I am infuriated that he should dominate the women so. Who gives him the right? Why doesn't somebody stop him?

"We must stand up to him!" I shout as I approach my sisters.

"Are you crazy?" the older one asks indignantly.

"Just like you," another says. "You take one look at him and decide we ought to fight him. You haven't even been in a skirmish before, while we've all been wounded."

Yet another sister admonishes me: "Now aren't we being a little presumptuous!"

"Let none of us be cowards because of him," I shout. "I will go forth and engage him."

"You! You're only a young woman; besides he's been groomed his whole life for domination. Mark my word, you'll end up his servant."

"The God who delivers me from the beasts of the field will also deliver us from this man," I reply confidently. "I am ready to do battle!"

Convinced I need plenty of protection, my sisters clothe me in a coat of mail and put a helmet upon my head, leaving me so weighted down that I can hardly walk. In my hand they place a heavy sword.

"You would send me off to fight him like this, in the very kind of armaments he's accustomed to? That give him every advantage in our confrontation? Take it all off."

What am I doing? I keep asking myself as I head back across the valley, this time in the open. Only a short time ago, I wasn't even aware of his hold over so many. Everyone who knows me considers me sweet, certainly not the kind to take on a man like this.

Now I'm on my own. Foolhardy, my sisters say of me, for I head out across the wide valley without any defense. Not even experience. Yet someone must stand up to this despot. Surely there exists some way in which he is vulnerable.

My legs feel unsteady, my hands are shaking. Dear God, I was meant to care for sheep, to nurture them and protect them. I was meant for a quiet life of singing praises to you and playing my lyre. Certainly I was not meant for action such as this.

Or was I? Have you been increasing my strength all along, God? Nurturing my spirit in the calmness of the pasture, giving me understanding, building my resolve to destroy the fears my sisters live with?

As I draw closer, the man turns around and stares at me. What a monster I've vowed to take on!

There's still time to turn around, run away from his indestructible power. No, it is not indestructible, or God would not have given me the resolve to put an end to this man's arrogance and control. And he is, after all, only a man, one who has chosen to use his size and strength to intimidate and control others. He must be stopped.

"Hah!" he shouts as I draw close, his voice filled with condescension. "You are no match for me. Why you're not even suited up for battle."

"You come with all your earthly power," I say with firm voice, "with privilege that has protected you all these ages; but I come to you in the name of God, and it is God, not I, you are mocking.

You shall be brought down with truth, the truth of the stories of women of all generations."

He moves toward me, as if all he has to do is step on me. I want to run, but to run is to deny the power I have just claimed. To run is to accept defeat. To run is to turn away from God.

My legs planted firmly on the ground, my hands on my hips, I am amazed by the ease with which I look up into his eyes. With a calmness that astounds me, I declare, "In the name of God, I order you to quit using your size and position to dominate."

His response is to roar with laughter. But from among the women who surround him, one steps away and comes to stand beside me. Another comes, then another. Soon all of his servants flank me while he stands opposite us, alone. Suddenly his mirth leaves him, and the whole hilltop becomes silent, as if a quiet mist has settled.

In his eyes I detect the strength of our presence. I see from looking into them that he is disoriented. Frantically he begins to turn his head in every direction, as if looking for someone, just one woman to remain with him. Seeing none, he stumbles backward several steps, then stops to lean on his spear. As if reminded of its function, he picks it up and throws it in our direction. But his thrust is weak and the direction of his mark is far to our right. He reaches for the javelin, which hangs across his shoulders, and throws it. It too falls short, far to our left.

Thirty, forty women strong, we march now upon him. Frantically stepping back, he trips over a rock and falls to the ground with a crash.

Out here in the desert, we learn to live with mirage. That must explain why some women claim dominating giants no longer exist and others excuse exploitive behavior by saying, "They mean no harm."

I, on the other hand, continue to fight the giants. Many days I dream of returning to the pasture, writing poetry, and practicing my lyre by the brook. But once a woman has taken up the battle cry, once she's looked the enemy directly in the eye, she can never return to life as it was before.

As She Loved Her Own Soul

1 Samuel 18—2 Samuel 1

A strong affection binds David and Jonathan, King Saul's son. Meanwhile, David's military successes are sending the king into a jealous rage. Several times, in fits of madness, he tries to kill David. Later Saul and Jonathan are both slain in battle, which leads to David's being anointed king of Israel.

Such affection connects women too.

SOME SAID that an evil spirit had entered the queen's mind, making her turn in rage against everyone, even those who were most loyal. Others claimed that she had long been a furious woman but until now had been able to control herself. No one could predict when the spells might occur. One minute the queen would be calmly carrying out her duties; the next minute a dark cloud moved over her spirit, causing her to lash out at those nearby.

At the first sign of a bout, servants would rush to find Davida, urging her to come play the lyre. They would beckon Joanna, the queen's daughter, to speak words of consolation. The gentle strums and soothing words seemed to calm the queen's spirit, and she would sit on her throne, eyes shut, shoulders relaxed. Every now and then, though, her body would suddenly twitch and she would grab her spear. Before anyone had a chance to stop her, she would thrust it, most often at Davida. Fortunately the queen's aim was poor and Davida had quick reflexes.

A few in the court began to wonder if Davida herself might be the problem; maybe the queen was jealous. For there was something about the young woman that caused all who came near her to know that God had chosen her for greatness. Every task she attempted she did exceedingly well, from writing poetry to playing the lyre. And already, at a young age, she was triumphant in battle, slaying the enemy with javelin and the bow.

No one admired these qualities more than did Joanna. She looked upon Davida's beauty: her compact body, her smooth dark skin, her composed, regal bearing. She was in awe of Davida's quick mind and forceful words.

Davida returned the affection, finding in Joanna a spirit in harmony with her own. Joanna's status as the queen's daughter had not tarnished her; neither had she given in to the temptations that often accompany power and wealth. Joanna was Joanna: warm, courageous, generous.

But it was their mutual concern for Joanna's mother that sealed their love. As darkness dropped upon the queen's mind and those around her could see that she warred within herself, Davida and Joanna spent hours in her chamber.

Once the queen had finally been lulled to sleep, the two young women would stroll around the palace grounds, sharing secrets of the heart. The sorrow of one was felt by the other, while the laughter of one brought laughter to the lips of the other.

One night, when they had seen the queen to bed, the two walked in the jasmine-scented garden. In low tones they declared their love. Pledging that their souls would forever be bound together, they knelt beside each other, calling on God to bless the union of their spirits. As a symbol of her love, Joanna removed the royal robe and gave it to Davida, along with her sword and bow. By this gesture she demonstrated that her love for Davida was more important than someday becoming ruler of the nation. In response, though the royal robe now rested upon her own shoulders, Davida bowed before Joanna, swearing eternal loyalty and devotion.

Davida continued to triumph in battle, slaying enemies with her sword, delivering captives to the queen. In the streets people sang of her accomplishments and her ability to overpower enemies. More and more the queen turned her anger against the valiant young woman, claiming she was ambitious and intent upon taking over the throne. Davida, however, never wavered in her loyalty. All of her conquests were on behalf of her ruler.

One evening, in the royal chambers, Davida sang and strummed the lyre while Joanna sat nearby humming. The queen was asleep, head resting against her chest. Suddenly her head jerked up, her eyes glazed in madness. Joanna screamed as in one swift motion her mother grabbed the spear beside her and thrust it at Davida. While it yet quivered in the wall, Davida fled. This time the queen's aim had been dangerously close.

In the days that followed the queen acted calm, as if the event had brought release from the tension. She carried out her usual responsibilities and did not summon Davida to play the lyre; neither did Davida come to the palace.

With no idea of her friend's whereabouts, Joanna was sick with worry, refusing all food that was set before her. Neither could she sleep. Perhaps Davida had been in a battle and lay dead somewhere. Yet in the quiet of the night, when silence surrounded her, Joanna could hear Davida's voice assuring her that she survived.

During such a night a stranger slipped past the palace guards to deliver a message. The stranger would take Joanna to the heroic warrior. Disguised as a servant, she left the palace and followed her guide. In a cave in a distant hillside she found Davida. There by torchlight the two women held each other, their tears intermingling.

"What have I done?" Davida asked, as she stepped away and began to pace. "What am I guilty of? I am loyal to your mother, yet she wants me dead."

"It can't be so," Joanna said, though she had been nurturing the same fears. "She tells me everything that is on her mind, and she's said nothing about killing you. Why would she hide such a wish from me?"

"Because she knows of the affection between us."

For a moment, while neither spoke, the darkness of the cave seemed to swallow them. "I don't know," Davida finally said. "I don't know. But it is too great a risk for me to venture back to the palace."

She came to stand before Joanna, taking Joanna's hands in her own. "We have a sacred covenant, you and I. Will you not try to learn her mind and report to me?"

"If I learn that she intends evil, you know I'll tell you."

"I have an idea. Tomorrow is the first of the festival days, and your mother has invited me to sit at her table. But to be safe I'll hide here for a few days instead. If she sees that I'm not there, tell her I had to attend the celebration with my family. If she says it's all right that I'm gone, then I'm safe for now. But if she's angry . . . well . . . if she wants me dead, you must warn me.

"And promise me something more. Promise that if there is any guilt in me—if I unknowingly have committed treason or broken any of God's laws—you will kill me yourself rather than bring me to her."

"You know I could never kill you," Joanna said. "As I have already promised, if I learn that my mother wishes for your death, I will tell you."

There in the cave the two of them devised a plan as to how Joanna might communicate her mother's frame of mind. Davida would go to the field where they had often met and hide behind a pile of rocks. Joanna would go there to practice her archery and bring along a child to fetch her arrows. If Joanna said to the child, "Look, the arrows are on this side of you," then her mother was not angry, and it would be safe for Davida to appear. But if Joanna said to the child, "Look, the arrows are beyond you," Davida was to stay in hiding.

"Promise me this," Joanna said when it was time for them to part. "No matter what happens, you will never renounce our friendship."

"God has joined us in love forever," Davida said, embracing her.

On the first day of the festival, the queen appeared not to notice Davida's absence. Certainly, Joanna thought, her mother had no need to worry that her authority would be seized. She had, after all, been anointed by God, and God would protect her.

However, on the second day, the queen, seated beside Joanna at the long banquet table, arched an eyebrow and asked, "Why has Davida not come to the meal yesterday or today?"

Pausing to take a sip of wine, Joanna tried to sound indifferent. "She was called to attend the celebrations with her family."

The queen leapt to her feet. "You are the daughter of a perverse, rebellious man!" Her lips barely apart, her head shaking in fury, she continued, "You know, don't you, that as long as she lives, you will not inherit my throne. She is intent upon usurping our power." Then, pointing toward the door, she ordered Joanna, "Bring her to me, for she is to die."

All conversation stopped. Only the servants moved, silently taking away dishes while adding others. Now Joanna was standing, eye to eye with her mother. "Why should she be put to death?" she asked, defiance in her voice. "What has she done?"

Before the queen could answer, Joanna ran from the table, now with a rage of her own. Either way she would lose Davida. Through death, if her mother had her way, or through Davida's permanent exile from the royal household.

Following a sleepless night, she arose early and took a young girl to the field where she and Davida had agreed to meet. "Run and find the arrow that I shoot," she instructed the child. "Isn't it beyond you?" she soon called out. When all three arrows had been shot and gathered, Joanna handed them back to her assistant and with tears in her eyes told the child to take everything back to the palace.

As soon as the girl was gone, Davida came out from behind the pile of rocks. Overcome with grief, the women clung to each other and wept.

"Go in peace," Joanna finally whispered, recognizing that Davida dare not linger. "We have already sworn before God that God shall be between you and me, and between your descendants and my descendants. Forever."

They walked away from each other, Davida returning to her hiding place, Joanna taking slow steps toward the city.

After that day they saw each other only once. Seeing the future in a dream, Joanna ventured to her dear friend's hiding place.

"Don't be afraid," Joanna said, holding tightly to Davida's hand, "for I have learned through a dream that my mother will never find you. Someday you will be queen, and I shall be next to you."

But Joanna returned home knowing that in spite of her words of encouragement they would never meet again.

The news came to Davida that Joanna had been killed in battle and that the queen had taken her own life. Because Davida had once lived in the royal court and had remained loyal, she mourned the loss of her ruler.

She mourned even more the death of Joanna, to whom her soul would be forever bound. These were the words she sang as she played her lyre:

> Joanna lies slain upon thy high places.
> I cry for you, my sister Joanna;
> Delightful have you been to me;
> Your love to me was wonderful,
> Surpassing the love of any man.

The Mentor

1 Kings 17—2 Kings 2

Israeli King Ahab is so tolerant of Baal worshippers that he even has a temple built for the Canaanite god. The prophet Elijah, after trying to convince King Ahab that abandoning the one true God is a big mistake, boldly announces that a great drought is coming. After three years of dryness, Elijah challenges the priests of Baal in a contest, posturing his God against theirs to see which one will bring rain.

When all the other prophets have been killed, leaving Elijah the only one, God sends Elisha to learn from him. The two men are together when Elijah is taken up to heaven.

How important an experienced mentor is to a woman destined for leadership and greatness.

I'M URGING the oxen to move a little faster, when she appears from nowhere: a strange looking woman with unkempt hair, wearing tattered garments. She comes over and without a word drapes her shawl over my shoulders. I understand immediately. Understand that I have been chosen to be her successor. Understand that her wisdom will be passed on to me. If I pay close attention.

"I can't just disappear," I say. "I have to go tell my children and grandchildren goodbye, then I'll accompany you."

Later, when I've taken my leave from family and joined her, the two of us sit in her tent. There I tend to her needs. With aloe I massage her feet, which have thick calluses. She makes no sound of protest as I comb the tangles from her hair. She is tired, she tells me, bone tired of fighting People of Power. Tired of speaking Truth when nobody wants to hear. Then she sits with eyes closed as I sing softly. Once in a while her gnarled hand reaches over to pat mine.

"A shame to wait until the end," she finally says, "a shame not to have had you with me sooner. But you weren't prepared. A woman must have years of experience before she's ready to speak Truth. So you had to be older, had to have seen too much to be quiet any longer." She mumbles to herself, "No, she wasn't ready before.

"Once we begin speaking"—she's again directing her words to me—"they discredit us as crazy Old Women." For a moment the weariness leaves her face as her cracked lips turn upward into a half-smile revealing missing teeth. "I rather like that term, don't you, even refer to myself as one. Old Woman, to whom One God has shown things as they are. A woman who both observes"—she opens her eyes wide—"and speaks."

I am surprised when immediately after uttering these words, her shoulders relax and her chin drops to her chest. At the sound of her faint snore, I leave her side to prepare a simple meal of bread, goat cheese, and pomegranate. Upon my return she rouses from her nap and begins to eat what I had placed before her. She chews slowly, speaking at the same time.

"There aren't many of us left, you know, Old Women who speak Truth. People of Power go to great lengths to silence us, for Truth threatens to bring them down. At first their strategy is to pay us no heed. 'They're only seeking attention,' they say. 'If we ignore them they'll go away.' Sometimes they laugh at us, confident that they can flirt with false gods and pillage One God's creation without consequences. They pass word around that what we see and speak of is the result of our imagination, not words from One God."

She pauses, chewing the bread while studying me intently. I study her too, think how beautiful she is, not because of youthful skin or curving body but because, in spite of her weariness, the spark in her eyes reveals wisdom and determination. I want my eyes to reflect hers.

She resumes talking: "There's one thing you should know before you commit yourself to becoming an Old Woman who speaks Truth. It is dangerous. I have often feared for my life, and People of Power have slain many sisters who refuse to remain silent."

Two tears escape the corner of her eye then follow a crease down her weathered face. I wonder what memory saddens her so but do not ask.

"Not long ago, when a large group of women proclaimed the Truth, People of Power set out to kill them all. One virtuous man—you may be surprised to know such men exist—when he learned they were to be annihilated, led a hundred women to a cave, where they lived on bread and water.

"And now you, one of the next generation, now it is time for you to take my place. The king still blames me for the drought, you know. I warned him the rains would cease—One God tells me these things, just as she will tell you. As soon as I delivered the message, I fled to the wilderness. It is not a good idea for an Old Woman to stay around when things aren't going well for People of Power. They blame *her*, when in fact they've brought misfortune upon themselves.

"Some time later, after the severe drought had been afflicting the land for quite some time, the word of One God came to me: 'Go present yourself to the king, and I will send rain.' Frankly, I was wishing One God would just send the rain and be done with it. I did not look forward to facing the king, for People of Power are prone to treat a woman my age as a public nuisance, whether we bring good news or bad. Besides, I knew that the forecast of rain did not mark the end of One God's displeasure.

"'So it's you, Old Woman, bane of our people,' the king shouted, drawing himself up to his full height to make me appear smaller. Then he smirked."

She forms the sinister smile she attributes to the king. I see renewed energy in her manner, whether from the nourishment of our meal or from reminiscing, I do not know.

"I could tell he had no intention of taking me seriously. I put my hands on my hips, I did, and lifted myself on my tiptoes. 'Am I the one who has turned to false gods?' I thundered. 'The drought has not come because of anything I've done but because you have forsaken the commandments.'

"Then—I'm rather pleased with myself, though it was One God's idea. You probably know already that if there's one thing People of Power cannot resist, it's rivalry. They assume that since they possess so much power, they can outsmart, outplay, outmaneuver any opponent. So right then and there I proposed a contest. The king and his priests would call upon their god, and I would call upon One God. You could see the arrogance on their faces as they agreed that the one to answer with fire was the true God.

"Oh, what a grand time that was," she tells me, clapping her hands in delight. "How glorious to show the might of One God. Laugh, I never laughed so hard in my life as I did while I watched them praying to their god, calling on it to bring fire upon the sacrifice.

"'Cry louder,' I taunted; 'Maybe your god is off somewhere thinking, or maybe he's gone on a trip. Maybe he's off taking a leak.' They didn't like that, my suggesting that their god might have such needs to attend to. Accused me of being irreverent, they did. But that's one of the advantages of becoming an Old Woman. You don't have to honor any god but your own.

"Then after nothing happened, when there was no sign of their god, and I'd had a good laugh, I called the people to gather around me. Just to add to the challenge, I told them to pour water all over the offering I'd prepared. Which of course annoyed them, the drought and all, my wasting water. But I kept assuring them that One God was going to make it rain.

"So there I stood—ah, the presumption of this job—an Old Woman standing before all those hostile people, and I called out as loud as my voice could shout, 'Oh God, answer my request, that all the nation will know you are One God.'"

She merely sits before me, silent, her eyes glistening

"What happened?" I finally ask.

"What would you expect, an Old Woman calling on One God for fire?"

"Fire?"

"Exactly. Why you never saw anything like it. Whoosh, down it came and just like that consumed everything on the altar, even the stones. Not long after that, clouds appeared in the west, then the thunder began to roll and rain started pouring from the skies."

She closes her eyes and is quiet again. But she continues to smile to herself. Is she picturing the flames dropping onto the altar, or the pouring rain, or the look on the king's face?

After a while she opens her eyes and looks directly at me. "People of Power say I have a problem with my anger, that I'm too confrontational. That's how they maneuver; they turn things around and create a lie that serves their purposes. The problem is *my* anger. Yes, I am an angry Old Woman, no denying that, but not nearly as angry as One God, who the People of Power provoke every day. They abuse creation, they wield their power with disregard for both One God and for the nation. They'll do anything to add to their coffers and their might. If they think I am angry, whooee, mine is nothing compared to One God's wrath!"

I have come to love her as my own mother. An ornery Old Woman she is, who aggravates People of Power by laughing at their excesses and their transitory symbols of might. She is right, I am ready, for in my later years I can no longer be seduced by their strutting and bravado. With age, I have discovered, comes freedom. What does an old woman have to fear? Not death; it is not far off anyway. Not public humiliation; that is a concern for youth.

This is my calling, to speak as she does, not what People of Power want to hear, but Truth. This is my calling, to hear the words of One God and to convey those words. I am learning to be like her, paying careful attention, learning what I must do to make sure One God's wishes are respected.

We are making our way down the road when we come upon the king's messengers resting by a spring. When she asks where they are going, they say they are on their way to ask prophets of their gods for signs of the future. After she chides the messengers for seeking counsel from those who know nothing, she tells them, "Take this message to the king. One God says he is going to die." They appear startled, not knowing whether to laugh at her or take flight.

The news must have caused the king to worry, for we're sitting at the top of a hill, waiting for the words of One God, when fifty soldiers arrive. Their captain announces, "Old Woman of One God, the king says 'Come down.'" She gives the captain a piece of her mind, telling him that the wishes of the king are not more important than our waiting for One God to speak. But the captain makes it clear he has no regard for what an Old Woman thinks she should or should not be doing at any particular moment. The king says come; she is to come.

"If I am a woman of One God," she finally shouts in exasperation, "let fire come down and consume you and your troops." Immediately fire descends, and flames surround them all. The same thing happens again with another captain and another group of soldiers. But when a third captain comes with fifty soldiers, he approaches with respect, and instead of ordering her to go to the king, he invites her.

Meanwhile, I am paying careful attention, learning what it takes to have my wishes respected.

We go to the king's court, not because the captain has been civil, but because Old Woman personally wants to give the king the news: He's going to die because he's rebuffed One God.

It's all quite amazing to witness: Old Woman's strength as she reproaches one as powerful as the king. He's accustomed to winning and certainly doesn't believe that Old Woman, even if she has the backing of One God, could be much of an adversary. He is wrong.

I accompany her everywhere, laboring to keep up with her when she feels vigorous, allowing her to lean on me when she's weary. I do not let her out of my sight, so fearful I am that she will soon die. Wherever we go women gather, oft times asking for advice, sometimes silently standing or sitting nearby in reverence.

One day she tells me, "Tarry here, for One God has sent me to the river." In her tone I hear resignation, and suddenly I fear that this leave-taking is to be our farewell.

I refuse to let her out of my sight. "As long as you live I shall not leave you."

So together we walk toward the river. The many women who have been respectfully following us stay behind a good distance, as if they too know that we are about to lose her.

She removes her cape, rolls it up, and strikes the water. The water parts, allowing the two of us to walk to the other side.

On the opposite bank she turns to me. "Tell me what I shall do for you before I am taken away."

"I pray that you will let me inherit a double share of your spirit."

Her laugh is not one of mockery but of gentleness. "You have asked a difficult thing; yet if you see me as I am taken away, you will have your wish. But if you do not see me go, your wish will not be granted."

We stand there speaking quietly, saying our farewells. I tell her how grateful I am that she has been my mentor and how I will never forget the days we've spent together. She assures me that I'm well on the way to becoming a wise Old Woman myself, and as long as I listen to the voice of One God rather than to the wishes of People of Power, I'm going to do well. I assure her that once a woman claims her power, she can't move backward. Be careful anyway, she says.

I am crying, and she is wiping away my tears. I clasp the shriveled, gnarled hand that rests upon my cheek.

Suddenly I hear the strong upward draft of an inferno, and I see that a chariot of fire and horses of fire have come between us. Before we have a chance to say more, she is lifted into the clouds and a whirlwind carries her and the chariot away.

"My mother, my mother," I call after her. But she is gone.

Throwing myself on the ground, my head against my knees, I sob. Never have I loved a woman more. Never have I witnessed her combination of humor and warmth and strength. And irreverence over the follies of People of Power. A double share of her spirit, I asked for, yet how can there ever be another woman like her?

As I lift my head I notice her cape, which must have fallen as she was being taken away. I fold it as she did earlier and touch the water, shouting, "Where is her One God?"

The waters part and I walk to the other side. The women who have been waiting nearby come to meet me.

More than a Woman Can Bear

Book of Job

With God's permission, Satan casts multiple hardships on Job: the loss of his children and possessions, physical afflictions. Three of Job's friends come by to offer their condolences but end up doing all the talking and offering advice.

When women face tragedy, we need friends who will simply sit with us—without theologizing and lecturing.

> Oh, God, who shall dwell with you?
> She who walks blamelessly, and does what is right,
> And speaks truth from the heart;
> Who doesn't slander with her tongue and
> Does no evil to a friend, nor criticize her neighbor.
> God, I trust that you will never turn away a woman
>   like this (Psalms 15).
>
> You bless the righteous woman;
> You cover her with favor as a shield (Psalms 5).

SUCH WERE yesterday's songs. Sung when I counted on God's continued blessings. Now the words are lodged in the back of my throat, with only an occasional *I praise your name* making its way to my lips. Spoken so faintly that even God can barely hear.

Losses almost too great to bear. My children are still young—no, they *were* young, already with skills and wisdom that benefitted others. My daughters have grown to be respected leaders—no, they *were* respected. They are, they were, they are, they were. How strange, in such a brief time to so drastically shift my thinking from present to past. To accept what could never be as what is.

My children—each carried in my womb, nurtured at my breast, lifted up to God in hope and love and joy. Welcomed into this world by aunts, uncles, cousins, neighbors, and of course father and mother. From the moment of their birth we nurtured them. For what purpose?

Better they had never been born.

Tears, where are the tears, people wonder. I ask the same question. Why am I not allowed the release that comes with tears? No, numbness is my state of mind, for my spirit cannot bear to feel the sorrow.

At the wrong place at the wrong time, people say. *Catastrophe,* it is called, as if that alone explains all that happened, as if God is capricious. Catastrophe. The word used by an observer to explain events, an utterance by one outside the circle of love. It is a word for others, not for me.

The word suitable for me? *Naked,* perhaps, for I have been stripped of everything that makes my life worthwhile. It is a harsh sounding word, *naked.* Naked I came from my mother's womb, and naked shall I return. God gives and God takes away.

Blessed be your name, oh God.

I have fallen down steep precipices before; I have had cuts across my flesh, and bruises. But no injuries to the body compare with the pain of sores that itch and burn and collect puss. I can do nothing but sit among the ashes holding a potsherd, which I use to scrape these terrible blisters covering me from head to foot.

"Curse God," my husband says, himself angered by the misfortune that has descended on us. I spurn his suggestion, for never in my life have I presumed to curse God. But life was good before, and God was to be praised for all my blessings. I thought myself protected, assuming I was being rewarded for my faithfulness.

Now I see that it is far easier to praise God when all is going well. When fortune changes—ah, then it becomes a different matter.

Accept reality and curse God, my husband repeats. How can I accept reality when it shifts so abruptly? When one day I am a woman of wealth and health, surrounded by people I love, and the next day all is erased? That is the nature of reality, I suppose: the possibility that everything can change so drastically, so suddenly.

Would I have been better off living in fear of such a time, careful not to love my children too much lest they be taken from me? Careful not to enjoy life too much lest my health and possessions be jerked away?

Accept reality, curse God. I could never confront God.

Friends, three of them, sit beside me. Their presence comforts me. There is no need for any of us to speak words in this pit with walls too steep for one with my now-frail body to climb out of. Only wait for my death.

It is far easier, I now see, to be the one offering friendship than the one receiving it. I worry my friends take too much time from their responsibilities. I blame myself for filling their hearts with gloom.

A wonderful friend, people used to say of me, always there for others. Now with three women beside me, I see the deficiency of my offerings, the inadequacy of tears shed on behalf of another's sorrow. I believed I understood when I did not. How easy it is to sympathize when the pain is another's; how easy to lift a prayer.

These women seated beside me, though they do their best, cannot know the sorrow of losing children, for they have lost none. They cannot know of the despair that comes with losing one's possessions, for they will return to the comfort of their homes, to security. They cannot know the grinding away of the spirit that comes with having one's health stolen.

They cannot know, just as I never knew.

The fourth day and I have not died.

How does a woman rank her adversities? Could someone in my situation claim one to be worst? And the next almost as bad but not quite? And the next? At times I think that if my children were alive, I could endure the other afflictions. But could I? What if all our possessions were destroyed and we had no shelter, no food? What if I had my children and we had our possessions, yet these sores covered my skin so that I was ugly in their eyes or in such misery that our times together could never be joy-filled?

I curse the day I was born, for my very birth is a mockery. An infant coming out in false hope. I should have been buried in the ground that day, my flesh rotted by now, my bones decayed. Better never to have flesh at all than have it give me constant misery.

Seven days and seven nights, and still death has not rescued me. Why is life prolonged for those who desire its end and denied those who welcome it?

My friends, now weary of silently waiting for death to overtake me, have begun to talk. At first they attempt cheerful chatter, friendly gossip about our neighbors, as if discussing the ordinary lives of others might cheer me. Quickly they see the futility. Now they seem to think they can help me by speculating on the actions of the one who gives life and takes it away.

"God is testing your faith. You must trust that God will heal you." How many times since all these calamities began have I turned to God and prayed that this pain would be removed from my heart, from my body?

"We cannot always understand God's ways, but be assured, God does have a reason for these afflictions." She is right, I don't understand. Certainly I have committed no offense so evil that it would bring down the wrath of God to such an extent.

"Think of it this way," the third friend says, rising to her feet so that the taut crusty skin on my neck cracks as I gaze upward, "The woman God censors, why she is blessed. You are blessed.

God wounds, but then God heals. Everything is going to turn out all right. You're going to live to be an old woman."

Some comfort. Who, after losing all that is precious to her would want to live so long? Breathing and feeling my own heart pump are of no value when the reasons for living have been taken away.

After a while all I hear is the droning of their voices. I concentrate on running the potsherd up and down my legs, trying to relieve the unbearable itching, scraping away the puss before it hardens.

How can a woman live with hope when the poison of God's arrows flows through her body? Which is worse, sorrow that poisons the mind or sores whose puss collects and spreads the venom? If only I could use the sharp edges of the potsherd to scrape away the puss that has gathered in my mind. Not a remedy, I know, but at least I would be doing something. To merely sit and wait for healing is futile.

"You're so strong," my friends tell me, admiration in their voices. I'm tired of being a strong woman. Those handed such misery should be granted superhuman stamina. Instead I am a mortal woman who must bear afflictions no mortal woman can endure. It would be far easier to lie down and die than hold on to life.

And if I cannot die, please God, at least bring me a friend who does not exploit my misfortune. Give me one who will relieve me of this burden of being strong and bring an end to the constant draining of my spirit. For I am the one propping up my friends, letting them use my woes to pursue their lust for dialogue. It is as if my situation has provided a complex puzzle that challenges their intellect. They seem energized by my maladies; my pain gives them reason to befriend me.

I need a friend who will offer no advice, make no attempt to interpret my woes, say no words of false comfort. I need a friend who will be with me and hold my repulsive looking hand.

Though three women sit beside me I feel lonely.

Daytime is wretched enough, but the nights are endless. It is in the nighttime that the memories hover and the voices of those I loved speak to me. I hear my daughters' and sons' laughter and recall a conversation, a tenderness that passed between us.

But it is also in the night that I remember an argument, a time when I demanded that a mother's wishes and wisdom be honored. I remember words of accusation that cannot be taken back. How I wish I had taken greater care in the words I chose, closed my lips until I was certain I had the right ones.

Yes, at night I hear the words. Over and over they come to me, some of them sweet and gentle, some strident. For a moment one of my daughters stands by me, and I reach out to touch her, but she disappears.

The nights—when the itching and aching of my sores intensify, keeping me from sleep. The long, long nights when God has sealed away the stars and the moon. When there is no light, only terrifying darkness.

Oh, that I could return to earlier days when God watched over me, when God's light guided me through the darkness and my children surrounded me. I appeared in public, and young women stepped aside; those my age nodded in respect. Neighbors listened to me and heeded my counsel.

Now they make fun of me, women and men much younger than I. They hate me and spit when they walk by the pit in which I languish. Even young children laugh at me and mock my name.

As long as a woman prospers, she has many friends. Let misfortune overtake her, and they disappear.

I suppose I should be grateful for the three who continue to pass off their collection of nonsense as wisdom.

"You've got to quit feeling sorry for yourself," one says. "Put a smile on that face." They would seem to prefer a fake smile to the truth of my condition.

"All of this will make you a stronger woman," says the one who only yesterday held up my strength as a virtue. What woman would choose to pay such a price for strength, I want to know. And of what benefit will it serve if all who need my strength have been taken from me?

The third friend tells me, "Don't let all of this turn you into a bitter woman." I'm not to be bitter? How much is a woman supposed to endure before she's allowed to become furious? If I am created in God's image, why am I not allowed wrath like God's? In fact, by comparison my fury seems harmless. It does not call forth a strong wind or a flood that destroys. My anger does no one any harm.

I have been betrayed. God, whom I honored, turned against me. Am I supposed to say, "That's quite all right." Who is not enraged when betrayed by a friend?

I'm tired of these three assuming that dissecting and scrutinizing the ways of God will help me. "If you would only do such and such," they tell me, "God would. . . " They furnish answers, craftily devising them, when I would rather they stammer and fret with me to find the right questions.

Questions need no answers, for it is in questions themselves that we grasp truth's complexity. My friends could sit around for years, no doubt, postulating answers when the right questions have never been asked.

If I were you, if I were you, if I were you. . . I never asked, "What would you do if you were in my situation?" And though they speak with confidence, pretending to impart God's thoughts, God's wisdom, God's reasons, I recognize their words as hollow. As healers they are worthless.

I should be grateful they remain with me.

I can restrain myself no longer; I will speak in the anguish of my spirit.

You, God—yes, I'm talking to you. It is with you, not these three women, that I want to argue my case. Why do you test me? I have tried to live a virtuous life. Have I not eased the suffering of the poor and helped the motherless who had no one else to depend on? I was eyes to the blind, feet to the lame, mother to the poor.

I relied on you to keep my family and me safe, to satisfy our needs. I turned to you as friend and companion, found comfort in your presence. As much as I put my faith in your steadfastness, I now see that you are not to be trusted. What kind of god delights in suffering as you do? What kind of god throws darts of destruction and disease at those who are faithful?

My friends insist I not be angry at you. If you do not like my rage, come to me directly and make an effort to reach an understanding. You have made my soul bitter, and if I denied my anger toward you, I would be lying.

You watcher of women and men, you have escaped to the heavens to avoid gazing upon my sores and hearing my cries of despair. Well, I have this to say to you: I will go bury myself in the earth, and you'll look for me, but I will fool you, for I shall have ceased to be.

My friends gasp in astonishment. How dare I, a woman, confront God Almighty? How dare I, a woman, argue with God and defend myself? How dare I suggest that God is wrong and I am right?

How dare I, a mere woman!

A Sisterhood of Survivors

Daniel 1–3

Upon the defeat of Judah, Nebuchadnezzar, king of Babylon, takes home some of Judah's most promising boys, among them Daniel, Hananiah, Mishael, and Azariah. (The latter three are today remembered by their Babylonian names: Shadrach, Meshach, and Abednego.) When, as adults, Shadrach, Meshach, and Abednego refuse to bow down to a golden image of Nebuchadnezzar, they are thrown into a fiery furnace. God, however, spares their lives.

Many women living under oppression have had the courage and strength to stand up to tyrants.

THEY MET regularly. In secret. Four young women. Arriving separately, they would make their way through a narrow passage to a recessed doorway, up a dark flight of stairs.

The brightness and elegance of the room they entered contrasted sharply with the shadowy stairwell. Mishael had creatively decorated it with colorful thick carpets and pieces of art she clandestinely made as reminders of the land of their birth.

"Take the enemy's loveliest and most intelligent girls back to our country," The Great Conqueror had ordered a servant many years earlier. Danile, Hannah, Mishael and Azari had been pulled from their mothers' sides and taken to a distant land. There they grew up receiving a superior education and comforts that surpassed anything they could have expected in their homeland.

Since The Great Conqueror did not like to hear foreign names and languages, she gave them new names in her language and ordered them not to speak their native tongue. Ever. In these ways, by changing their names and denying them their language, did The Great Conqueror try to deprive the girls of their true identity.

No doubt she assumed they would eventually forget former loyalties and become her faithful servants. But it is not easy to dominate the mind of an intelligent girl, not simple to make sure she thinks and speaks and acts like her oppressor. Especially when she has a circle of friends who encourage her to stay true to herself and her heritage. Danile, Hannah, Mishael and Azari continued to remind each other in whispered tones they were daughters of God in Heaven.

Thus it came about that these four foreign girls grew to be young women. And it was as wise women that they now sat on the rugs of their secret room sharing a simple meal.

Azari, the youngest, had been barely eight when brought to this land. Though she had become a competent woman with weighty administrative responsibilities, the others still tended to mother her. She did not mind, for a woman on whom others rely also needs someone to lean on.

Though all had remained faithful to God in Heaven, the four could not have done so without Mishael's strong faith and assurance that if they did what was just and noble, God in Heaven would protect them. She inspired the others with her creativity and insight.

Hannah was the loveliest, with beautiful brooding eyes and a complexion that belied the harshness of the climate. Able to remember the sacred stories her mother and father had told her as a young child, she recited the narratives that helped sustain these exiles.

Of the group, Danile had gained the most prominence. In addition to a keen intellect, she had the gift of interpreting dreams, which elevated her in The Great Conqueror's eyes and earned Danile a permanent place in the royal court. Because of her extraordinary ability, she had been able to bargain for positions of responsibility for her three friends.

To others the four appeared to be young women of power. Their influential jobs, exquisite garments, and sophisticated bearing suggested control over their own destinies. However, in reality, their power, like that of even the native-born, depended upon the whims of The Great Conqueror, who exercised vicious domination over her subjects' every action.

In this room the four women could converse with honesty. In their native tongue, calling each other by their birth names, they were able to speak of their sorrow over never again seeing their families and homelands. They could share memories of their mothers and fathers, sisters and brothers, and worship God in Heaven together, reciting prayers they remembered from early childhood. They could condemn The Great Conqueror's statutes.

Upon The Great Conqueror's announcement, the women hastily made their way to the secret room. All but Danile, who was attending to business in another part of the kingdom.

They should have anticipated the problem, they agreed. It wasn't as if the giant statue had been hidden from view while being built. No, there it stood, out on the wide plain for all to see: a golden likeness of The Great Conqueror. Had confidence in their important status blinded them to its significance?

Today had come the announcement: "Upon the sound of the horn, the lyre, the harp, and the bagpipe, the governors, the magistrates, and all officials of all the provinces are to bow down and worship the statue."

Arms waving in gestures of agitation, the three young women began talking at once, moving back and forth between the language of their heritage and that of their oppressors. Until Mishael put her index finger to her lips as a reminder that they dare not be heard by neighbors.

Hannah was angry. She clinched her fists and gritted her teeth. "I hate her! I hate her! I hate her! Vain, selfish. She's evil, that's what she is, evil."

Azari was terrified. She pressed her hands to her cheeks and choked on her words: "We're going to die. A fiery furnace. We're going to die in a fiery furnace."

Few words inspire more than those conveying profound trust in God in Heaven. So when Mishael reached over to place a hand on Azari's shoulder, when Mishael spoke from the heart of how God in Heaven had protected them in the past from the whims of The Great Conqueror, and would protect them again, her two friends recognized the truth of her words.

Which didn't necessarily comfort them.

"Even so, we must decide what to do," Hannah said.

Azari nervously fingered the gold hoop in her ear. "I say we do as the decree says. Surely that's what God in Heaven expects. So we'll be safe from The Great Conqueror's wrath."

"People here are accustomed to worshipping many gods," Hannah said, "and we would be showing respect for their ways. I agree with Azari. It is what God in Heaven wants us to do, obey the law."

As Azari and Hannah built a case for bowing to the golden statue, Mishael stood and began pacing the narrow room, at the same time playing with the fringe of her scarf. Finally she reminded them, "If we do, we will be breaking God in Heaven's commandment not to worship other gods."

Azari and Hannah spoke in unison: "But we wouldn't be worshipping in our *hearts.*"

Mishael stopped pacing and knelt before them. "God in Heaven will not abandon us now. We must not break her commandment."

No one spoke for a while, each woman absorbed in her own thoughts about what to do.

Hannah's eyes lit up. "I have an idea. What if—that big crowd of people, everyone bowing. Everyone's face will be to the ground. When they all start to bow, what if we look like we're going to but—"

"You mean only do it part way?" Azari asked.

Like a scolding mother, Mishael wagged her finger. "We were taught to bow down to no other god. Surely that includes a half-bow."

It grew late, and still the three had not reached consensus. Azari thought they should obey the edict; Mishael was convinced they should not; Hannah held on to the hope that God in Heaven would intervene before they were forced to decide.

The day of great importance arrived. The wide plain was crowded with governors, magistrates, and every official from every province. The signal came: the sound of the horn, the lyre, the harp, and the bagpipe. Around Hannah, Mishael and Azari the multitude began to lower themselves to the ground.

Hannah looked at Azari, who was trembling in fear. Azari looked at Mishael, who was staring at the giant golden statue looming over the entire plain. Azari rearranged her robe and bent her knees as if preparing to fall to the ground. Hannah lowered her body slightly and leaned forward from the waist. Of the three, only Mishael appeared confident of what God in Heaven required. Standing straight, hands to her side, chin thrust forward, she turned her eyes from the statue and lifted them skyward.

It was at that moment that Azari saw her mother's eyes, filled with sorrow as they'd been the day The Great Conqueror's servant had taken the girls away. Only now they expressed grief over her daughter choosing to forsake God in Heaven. As Azari straightened her knees she lifted a silent prayer. When Hannah saw that Azari and Mishael both stood, she too straightened, knowing that by doing so she sealed her doom.

By now everyone else lay prone before the golden statue of The Great Conqueror. Everyone but the three young women.

There were many in the land who envied the success of the three young women. "It is because those foreigners have flattered The Great Conqueror that they have gained such high status," they said to each other. "Our own citizens are as knowledgeable as they, yet none of us gets the prestigious jobs." "Why doesn't The Great Conqueror promote some of our own people over them?" "The foreign women should be sent back to their own country, better yet, killed."

The jealous people reported to The Great Conqueror, "When the time came to bow down to the golden statue, three women with prominent positions in the affairs of state ignored your command."

The Great Conqueror became angry and called Hannah, Mishael, and Azari before her. "Why must you defy me?" she shouted. "I have given you jobs of importance, elevated you even over my own people. You should be grateful. I will tell you once more: When you hear the sound of the horn, the lyre, the harp, and the bagpipe, you are to bow down to the image. If you do not, I will have you thrown into a fiery furnace."

The three women stood calmly before The Great Conqueror. Mishael spoke on the others' behalf: "We trust that God in Heaven, God of our tradition, will deliver us from the fiery furnace. But if not, know that we will not serve your gods or worship the golden image you have set up."

"I am the one you serve!" The Great Conqueror screamed. "Only I have the power to deliver you from the fire!" And to the servant she commanded, "Prepare the furnace. Make it seven times hotter than I told you before!"

Hannah, Mishael, and Azari had no chance to speak with each other. Bound tightly in their clothes to prevent them from moving their limbs, they barely had time to utter a prayer to God in Heaven. The Great Conqueror's servant led them into the furnace with heat so intense that the flames immediately killed the servant.

A short time later, satisfied that her mandate had been carried out, The Great Conqueror peered into the furnace. She was amazed to see not three, but four women walking in the midst of the flames. Awe-struck, she described the fourth woman as having the appearance of the "daughter of the gods."

So God in Heaven protected the three wise young women, leading The Great Conqueror to proclaim, "Blessed be the God of Hannah, Mishael, and Azari!"

Thus it came about that they were promoted to yet higher positions in the government.

They are old women now. Mishael is no longer living, buried in the sands of this land far from her place of birth. The other three still meet in the room, which because of The Great Conqueror's proclamation, no longer needs to be a secret place. There they speak of Mishael's faithfulness to God in Heaven and feel her spirit in their midst.

Few things are more precious to a woman than friends who understand her. Danile, Hannah, and Azari value each other partly because within this room are the only people who have known them since childhood. What a precious gift a lifelong friend is.

As older women they now have an additional reason for needing each other: Together they are able to combine their memories to create a coherent history. When their thoughts skip around, when one forgets a detail, the others provide the missing information.

The three women are part of a sisterhood of survivors, women who have lived under tyranny and oppression. Lived either near the heart of power or on the fringes of society. Some, such as Danile, Hannah, Mishael and Azari, are foreigners; some are daughters of the oppressors. Survivors have kept the stories alive, stories about how women, in spite of hardship, have remained faithful to God in Heaven.

So that we too may find courage.

The Nice Woman

Jonah 1–3

When the prophet Jonah is told by God to go to Nineveh and cry out against its wickedness, he balks and gets on a ship, hoping to escape the presence of God. God causes a great storm that threatens the ship. The sailors finally understand that Jonah is the cause of the terrible storm and at his insistence throw him overboard. He is swallowed by a great fish in whose belly he stays for three days and three nights. Once the fish spews Jonah out, Jonah does as God commands: He goes to Nineveh, rails against its evil ways, and inspires the people to repent.

Boldly confronting sin can be difficult for women, who have been taught from childhood to be nice.

Jonah means Dove.

DOVE GAVE the goat to her best friend, packed all her belongings in a single satchel, and caught the first freighter for Tarshish. She was trying to escape the presence of God.

As she stood on deck watching the shoreline fade from view, God's message echoed in her mind: "Go to the city of Nineveh and speak against it for its wickedness." *Speak against it for its wickedness, speak against it for its wickedness.*

A rather distasteful demand, considering what a nice woman Dove was. For her attitude was always positive. "There are no bad people," she was known to say, "only bad deeds." Why the very thought of denouncing a whole city for its wickedness upset her digestive system and gave her a terrible headache. Furthermore, she had never been to the city and had no desire to go, for cities were dirty and she much preferred cleanliness. Besides, someone was certain to take advantage of a woman as delicate and gentle-natured as Dove. Not that the people in Nineveh were bad, of course, but she knew they did sometimes resort to bad deeds.

Tarshish probably would not be much different. But maybe God wouldn't be able to find her there, and she wouldn't have this heavy responsibility hanging over her. She could remain her sweet self.

Go and speak against it for its wickedness. An assignment grim enough to send any woman into flight. But of course a woman can't escape God so easily, and God is upon the sea as well as upon the land, in one city as much as in another.

While Dove tried to journey away from the presence of God, God sent a great storm over the sea. Even though the ship swayed and bounced upon the roaring waves, even though the water swept over the deck causing all on board to fear the boat would break in two, Dove kept her optimistic disposition. "I'm sure everything will turn out all right," she told the others. To prove her confidence, she went below and took a long nap. Meanwhile, the sailors began to throw the ship's cargo overboard.

As the storm continued to intensify, the crew shouted above the howl of the wind, appealing to their own gods. Still the sea raged. "Whose fault is this evil?" they asked among themselves. Determining that the storm had something to do with Dove, they went below and shook her shoulders. "Who are you?" they demanded to know, "and what did you do, and why has this terrible storm come upon us?"

In spite of being so rudely awakened, Dove sat up and politely answered their questions. "I am Dove, and I am a nice woman and I always look for the best in people and everything's going to work out just fine."

"What is this you've done?" they again demanded.

The Nice Woman

Heaving a great sigh, she told them about not following God's directive, and about how she believed all people were basically good, but what God wanted went totally against her nature, so she was fleeing the presence of God.

Meanwhile, the sea grew more and more tempestuous, until finally Dove could not stand the thought that all on board would perish because she was avoiding the responsibility God had placed on her.

"Toss me into the water," she said.

Having never thrown a woman overboard, the crew at first protested. But only briefly, for they were convinced that the only way to save themselves was to do as she told them. Two quite muscular men took hold of her, one grabbing her arms, the other her feet, and with a one, two, three, they threw her overboard. Immediately the sea ceased its raging.

For the first time in her life Dove, who did not know how to swim, knew panic. As the gentle waves tossed her about, she thrashed her arms and tried to keep her head above water. Finally, however, the waters closed above her and weeds rose up from the depths to wrap themselves around her. Down, down they pulled until a great fish, appointed by God, swallowed her.

Now God had been in the seas and on the boat and in the bottom of the boat, but, Dove discovered, there was no sign of God in the belly of the great fish. She could no longer hear God urging her to go to Nineveh. All was darkness and silence.

Trying to make the best of a bad situation, as was her way, she sat in the fish's belly, thinking. She figured she had time to think.

It can take days for truth to come crashing down on a woman. For some women even longer. So accustomed was Dove to being adaptable and tolerant that a long stretch of darkness was necessary before she would be able to perceive what she had not been perceiving.

She had anticipated feeling liberated from the burden of God's expectations, but being inside the belly of the fish was not the respite she had expected. Her body was cramped, the walls of the fish's sides within reach from where she sat. And she was hungry. Gradually it began to dawn on her that this dark place would be her tomb. Better that she had gone to Nineveh and preached what she did not want to preach than to die here in the depths of the sea. Better to be loaded with a grim responsibility than have no future.

Her fear became anger. How dare God put such an impossible demand upon her! God knew her temperament, how ill-suited she was for such a task. How dare God let her die in such a dreadful way!

Then her anger turned to despair. Hope was now beyond her grasp, for hope is of God. Love was beyond her grasp, for love is of God. Strength was beyond her grasp, for it too is of God. She realized that no degree of looking on the bright side or trying to make the best of a difficult situation could compensate for the absence of God. Dove was utterly alone, and her loneliness terrified her.

So went her first day in the belly of the fish.

For the length of the second day she pondered what God had asked of her. *Go to Nineveh and cry against it for its wickedness.* Well, yes, people there had turned to other gods. And yes, they did not live according to the Commandments but stole from each other and lusted after each other's husband and wife and coveted their neighbor's house and did not honor their elders. The corruption of the people would surely destroy all sense of kinship and duty to each other.

On the third day Dove considered the problem of her own nature. Until now she had not known it was a problem. She had thought that God's request demonstrated God's inability to understand her. There in the darkness she perceived that in fact *she* was the one without empathy. By remaining cheerful she had detached herself from the sorrow God felt over the corruption of Nineveh. And now that she knew what the absence of God felt like, she understood what was in store for the people of Nineveh if she did not warn them. They would experience the loss of hope and cry out that they had been abandoned by God. When in fact they had abandoned God.

That night, at the end of the third day, there inside the giant fish, Dove broke out in song. Not a cheerful song as from earlier days but an honest song:

> You cast me into the deep because I would not listen,
> Would not listen to your instructions to journey to the great
> City and cry out against its wickedness.
> For I thought I knew human nature better than you
> And surely it was not appropriate for a woman to speak harshly.
> How can I both flee from you and flee toward you?
> Yet that is what I did, for you are God of the depths as well as
> God of firm land.
> You cast me into the deep, where the waves surrounded me.
> Down, down I descended
> Yet you brought me back, reached down and drew me upward.
> Those who pay homage to the vain idols of cheerfulness and smiles
> Deny their faith in a God who can be with the people in their sorrow.
> Now with a voice of thanksgiving I praise you for having
> Delivered me from myself.

Upon hearing this song, God spoke to the fish, which heaved and heaved then spewed Dove out upon the dry land.

"Arise, go to Nineveh," God instructed while she still sat on the sandy shore, her eyes barely accustomed to the light. "Proclaim the message that I tell you."

Dove had tried to be a nice woman for so many years that in spite of her new willingness to do as God commanded she was apprehensive over naming evil and speaking out against it. What good could she do God if people did not like her? Yet standing before a crowd of onlookers, her knees knocking, her stomach churning, Dove yelled out boldly, "Yet forty days, and Nineveh shall be overthrown!"

She was startled by the authority in her voice, the power of her presence. To her amazement, the people listened and believed her. They wept over their sins and asked for forgiveness. The king even commanded, "Let everyone turn from evil ways and from the violence which is in each hand."

So that when God witnessed the repentance of all, God too was remorseful and spared the people of Nineveh.

www.ingramcontent.com/pod-product-compliance
Lightning Source LLC
Chambersburg PA
CBHW071331190426
43193CB00041B/1564